Computer Network Algorithms
Implementation Using Scilab
First Edition

Dr.T.Subbulakshmi

September - 2017

Acknowledgement

I convey my special thanks to **Mr. G. Viswanathan**, Founder and Chairman, VIT University, TamilNadu, India for his encouragement and support. I would like to convey my special thanks to **Mr. Sankar Viswanathan**, Vice President, VIT University for his encouraging words. I am thankful to **Ms. Kadhambari S. Viswanathan**, Assistant Vice President, VIT University Chennai for providing a diligent ambiance of work. I am thankful to **Dr. Anand A. Samuel** for showing innovative digital pathway for achieving success in life. I am thankful to **Dr. N. Sambandam** for the sincere guidance and continued support. I am thankful to my Dean **Dr. Vaidehi Vijayakumar** and former Dean **Dr. L. Jeganathan** for providing happy work environment. I would like to thank Scilab NARVAL Module support team **Dr. Foued Melakessou** and **Dr. Thomas Engel** of University of Luxembourg for releasing the toolbox NARVAL and NTG. The author would like to thank **Mr. N. Udayakumar**, for his contribution towards LATEXcompilation and layout of this book.

This work was started as an embedded project component of the courses Advanced Computer Networks, Networks and Communication, Data Communications, Information and Cybersecurity, Information and system security. The students who have taken up these courses are interested in implementing the computer networks algorithm using Scilab NTG and NARVAL Toolboxes. The author has taken up the task of implementing the algorithms along with the students. The author would like to thank and extend heartfelt appreciation towards the following students for their consistent efforts

Name of the Program	Student Name
Degree Of The Graph	MEGHPAL SINGH
Distance Of Graph	
Edge Length	
Graph Connex	
2D Plot	
3D Plot	
Circle Plot	
Ellipse Plot	
Ellipsoid	
Mu Law	
Parabola	
Play Sound	

Sphere	
Toroid	
Error Correction	KUNI PREM KUMAR
Hamming Distance	
Minimum Hamming Distance	
3D Spline Interpolation	
ASCII Value Printing	ANKIT DUA
Dijikstra Network Topology	
Euclidian Distance	
Extract Largest Connex	
Generating Random Integers	
Plot 3D	
Discrete Calculation	SNEHIL BANERJEE
Topology Generation	
New Node Central	KAVATHIA HARSHAL GHANSHYAMBHAI
Plot Sin and Cos	VISHNU REMESH
Finding Largest Eigen Value Matrix	
Eulers Method For Solving IVP	
Integration Calculation	
Finding lowest and upper matrices	
Number of iteration matrix value	
Positive Root of the function	
RED and GREEN Matrix of Image	
Prime number checking	
Positive Root of the function	
Dynamic Equation	NEERAJ CHANDY KURIAN
Diagonalisation	
Inverse Laplace Transform Partial Difference	
Laplace Transform Partial Difference Calculation	
Subplot	
Bubble Sort	A M PRAJWAL
Insertion Sort	
Selection Sort	
Armstrong Number	SNEHA BANERJEE
Bisection	
Gauss Jordan Elimination	
Naive Gaussian Elimination	
Calculator	POTULA PAWAN KUMAR
Hamming distance	
Heart Shaped Curve	

BFS to a random source node and display the corresponding graphs	A.VIJITHA
Topology Creation For BFS	
Generation of topology in Barabasi Albert using BFS Plot	
Generation of topology using waxmanconnex	CHARISMA M
Generation of BFS weightplot graph for waxmanconnex topology	
Generation of locality connex	V.NIVEDHA
Generation of BFSWSearchStart for grid topology	
Generation of topology in barabasi alebert using DFS plot	K.SAIKEERTHI
Generation of topology in Multi-Level using DFS plot	
Generation of dfs search end for Waxman mode topology	A TEJA PRIYANKA
Generation of AddWaxman to Node topology	
Generation of waxmann using DFSWeightPlot	REGULA HARIPRIYA
Generation of DFSWeightPlot for Grid Topology	
Generation of DFSWeight for AddWaxman to Node Topology	
Nertwork Topology Creation using Waxman layer approach	TAMARANA ROHINI
Application of Routing FloydWarshall	
Application of BellmanFord	NEETIKA VERMA
Application of Dijkstra	
DFS Weight Plot	
Application of Prims	
One node to the closest Access Point in respect with multiple paths	KATTA SRUJAY
One node towards the closest Access Points	
One node towards all reachable Access Points	
Topology Creation and application of Routing Dijkstra	AKHILA THALLA
BellmanFord Shortest Path	
Comparison of Dijktras and Prims	

Edge Length of Nodes	
Implementation of floyd warshall routing algorithm for different topologies	ASHISH BENJAMIN ALAICHAMY
NtgLocality and NtgLocalityConnex	
Network topology generation Waxmann Comparison	
Routing Table optimization using Dijkstra	HIMANSHU, SAGAR THAKARE, SAKSHAM HANDU
RoutingTable Flood and Bellmanford	
Routing using BFS and DFS	
Weight graph generation	
Shortest path between two nodes using Dijkstra	
Floydwarshall algorithm Creation	
BellmanFord Comparison	DHRUV DIXIT, SACHIN GOPAL,GONDALIA AASHAY BATUKBHAI
BellmanFord Comparison Plot	
BFS Comparison	
BFS Comparison Plot	
BFS Weight Comparison	
BFS Weight Comparison Plot	
DFS Comparison	
BFS Comparison Plot	
DFS Weight Comparison	
DFS Weight Comparison Plot	
Dijikstra Comparison Plot	
Dijikstra Comparison	
FloydWarshall Comparison	
FloydWarshall Comparison Plot	
Gigantic Network Routing Performance	
Large Network Routing Performance	
Medium Network Routing Performance	
Prims Comparison	
Prims Comparison Plot	
Small Network Routing Performance	
Tiny Network Routing Performance	

VeryLarge Network Routing Performance	
Shortest path using Dijiktras	PRANAVCHENDUR T K
Shortest path using Prims	K V PRATHAP
Circle Place Comparison	MOHAMED AGHIL
Comparison of Dijikstra and Prims	
Analysis of Dijikstra	
Edgelength	
Enhanced Routing Table Vs Shortest Routing Table	
Euclidean Distance	
NTG Locality Connex	
NTG Waxmann Comparison	
Rounting Table Optimisation of Djkstrs	
Rounting Table BellmanFord	
Rounting BFS and DFS	
Vector Operation	
Weight Graph	
Visualization	SHIVADHWAJ SR,ANUBHAV SINHA

Dr.T.Subbulakshmi

Preface

This book has been compiled with the objective of explaining the basics of Scilab and Advanced Computer Network algorithm implementation using Scilab

Chapter one covers the introduction part with basic programming in Scilab such as graph plot, value printing , etc.,.

Chapter two discuss about the various network topology generation, simulation of routing algorithms and its comparative analysis.

Chapter three shows visualization techniques

I wish all the readers for a successful career in the field of Computer Networks Algorithms Simulation and Understanding.

About the author

Dr. T. Subbulakshmi is currently working as a Professor in the School of Computing Science and Engineering at VIT university Chennai Campus, Tamilnadu, India. Earlier she has worked as the Head, Department of Computer Science and Engineering, Sethu Institute of Technology, Virudhunagar,Tamilnadu, India and Assistant Professor in Thiagarajar College of Engineering,Madurai, Tamilnadu, India.

The author has contributed in framing many Computer networks and security based syllabus for engineering students like computer networks, information security, network security, cryptography, intrusion detection systems and cloud security. The author is actively taking part in most of the networks and security forums.

The author has also contributed in the complete curriculum design and development for M.Tech CSE with specialization in Information Security Program at VIT University Chennai. The author is a cloud certified associate from EMC2. The author used to conduct series of workshops for engineering and arts students in the area of Computer Networks.

The author has the experience of doing consultancy projects in security using open source security tools. The author has 16 years of experience in teaching and consultancy work. The author is involved in the design of new operating systems based on Linux Kernel based on mod security and member of the Special Interest Group on Operating Systems (SIG-OS).

The author has completed a project using Security tools in Linux Design of Masquerader Detection Systems for Information Security for Computer Society of India (CSI). The author has completed her research as a part of the Smart and Secure Environment Project, funded by National Technical Organization (NTRO),New Delhi.

The author is an expert in developing real time security policies based on open source tools and has publications in 16 Journals, 12 conferences, 3 magazines, two book to her credit. The author can be reached at subbulakshmibest@gmail.com

About the Book

Scilab is a scientific software package package that provides a strong open computing environment for engineering and scientific applications. Distributed freely via the net since 1994, Scilab is currently being used in academic and industrial environments around the world.

The objective of this book is to provide an intensive description of Scilab's use, as well as a way to master its environment and programming language, the utilization of integrated graphics, the incorporation of user-provided functions, and a tour of the many application toolboxes. Scilab is considered to be the wonderful alternative of Matlab which is a commercial one. The basic Scilab programs are extended to understand the Scilab programing language, routing algorithms, congestion algorithms, topology generation methods using NARVAL and NTG Toolboxes.

Network Analysis and Routing eVALuation toolbox is referenced as NARVAL and Network Topology Generator is referenced as NTG are designed on top of the Scilab environment. It has been created at the University of Luxembourg within the Interdisciplinary Centre for Security, Reliability and Trust (SnT). NARVAL permits to generate random topologies according to various algorithms such as Locality, Waxman, Barabasi Albert and hierarchical models. The user can also design his own topology by providing nodes' coordinates, visualization parameters, and also links' information that are necessary for path calculation. The combination of these functions enables to build a large range of topologies with distinct routing properties.

Contents

Chapter 1

Basic Programs

1.1 Circle Place

```
NumberOfNodes=500;
//original network size
L=1000;
//network square area side
dmax=100;
//Locality radius
[g]=NtgLocalityConnex(NumberOfNodes,L,dmax);
//generation of a topology in respect with the Locality method
gn=length(g.node_x);
//real network size
i=Random(gn);//selection of the central node
N=10;
//quantity of new nodes
d=50;
//disc radius
[ge]=CirclePlace(N,d,g,i);
//application of CirclePlace
ge.edge_color=[ones(1,length(g.head)) 5*ones(1,N)];//display
    the union graph
ge.edge_width=[ones(1,length(g.head)) 1.5*ones(1,N)];
ge.node_color=[ones(1,length(g.node_x)) 5*ones(1,N)];
//ge.node_color(i)=1;
ge.node_border=[ones(1,length(g.node_x)) 1.5*ones(1,N)];
//ge.node_border(i)=2;
show_graph(ge);
```

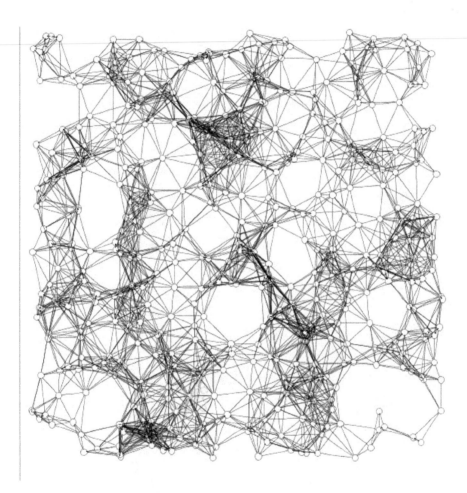

Figure 1.1: Circle Place

1.2 Degree Of The Graph

```
networksize=500;//network size
Maximum4Links=4;//a maximum of 4 links are created for any
    created node
NetworkSquareArea=1000;//network square area side
[topologygraph,degree]=NtgBarabasiAlbert(networksize,
    Maximum4Links,NetworkSquareArea);
//generation of the topology
show_graph(topologygraph);
[degree,dv]=GraphDegDistWD(topologygraph);
//application of GraphDegDistWD
```

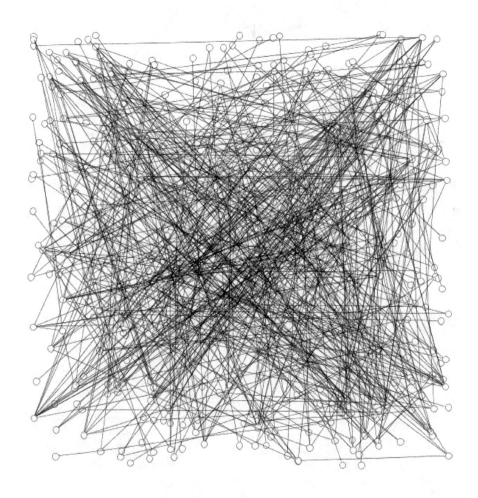

Figure 1.2: Degree of the Graph

1.3 Distance Of Graph

```
NumberOfNodes=100;//network size
SquareArea=1000;//network square area side
localityradius=100;//locality radius
[topology]=NtgLocalityConnex(NumberOfNodes,SquareArea,
    localityradius);//generation of a random topology in respect
    with the Locality method.
N=length(topology.node_x);//real network size
[n1,n2]=Random_i_j(NumberOfNodes);//selection of two distinct
    nodes
nd=ones(1,n);//display the graph
nc=ones(1,n);
nodediameter([n1 n2])=3;
nodecolor([n1 n2])=5;
show_graph(topology);
[d]=Distance(n1,n2,topology.node_x,topology.node_y);
//application of Distance
disp("Node 1=")
disp(n1)
disp("Node 2=")
disp(n2)
disp("Ditance")
disp(d)
```

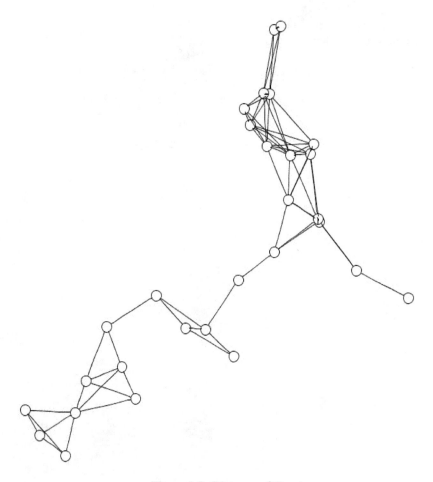

Figure 1.3: Distance of Graph

1.4   Edge Length

```
NumberOfNodes=50;//network size
networksquarearea=1000;//network square area side
dmax=100;//locality radius
[topologyGraph]=NtgLocalityConnex(networksize,networksquarearea
    ,localityradius);//generation of a random topology in
    respect with the Locality method.
show_graph(topologyGraph);
topologyGraph.edges.data.length=[]
[topologyGraph]=EdgeLength(topologyGraph);//application of
    EdgeLength
disp("Edge Values=")
disp(topologyGraph.edges.data.length)
```

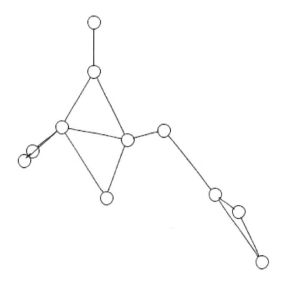

Figure 1.4: Edge Length

1.5 Graph Connex

```
networksize=50;//network size
networksquareareaside=1000;//network square area side
localityradius=100;//locality radius
[topologyGraph]=NtgLocality(-networksize,networksquareareaside,
    localityradius);//generation of a random topology in respect
    with the Locality method.
[topologyGraph1]=GraphConnex(topologyGraph);//application of
    GraphConnex
show_graph(topologyGraph);
show_graph(topologyGraph1)
```

Figure 1.5: Most Connected Graph

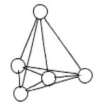

Figure 1.6: Connex in Connected Graph

1.6 2D Plot

```
x=0:0.05:5
y1=sin(x)
y2=cos(x)
y3=sin(x.^2)
y4=cos(x.^2)
plot(x,y1,x,y2,x,y3,x,y4)
```

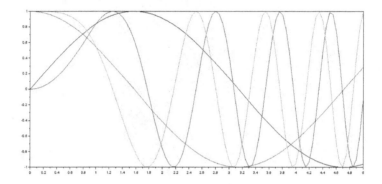

Figure 1.7: 2D Plot

1.7   3D Plot

```
t=[0:0.2:2*%pi]'
z=sin(t).^2*cos(t').^3
plot3d(t,t,z)
```

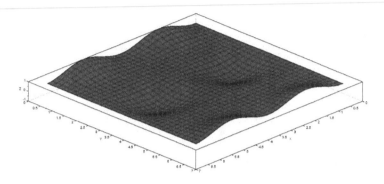

Figure 1.8: 3D Plot

1.8   Circle Plot

```
a = gca()
a.isoview = 'on'
xc = 0
yc = 0
r = 2
a = linspace(0, 2*%pi, 100);
x = xc + r*cos(a)
y = yc + r*sin(a)
plot(x, y)
```

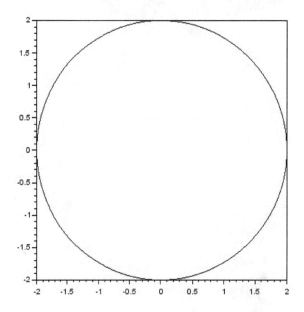

Figure 1.9: Circle Plot

1.9   Ellipse Plot

```
a = gca()
a.isoview = 'on'
xc = 0
yc = 0
r = 2
a = linspace(0,2*%pi, 100);
x = xc+6*cos(a)
y = yc+1*sin(a)
plot(x, y)
```

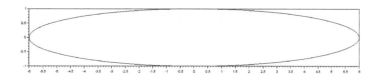

Figure 1.10: Ellipse Plot

1.10   Ellipsoid

```
u = linspace(-%pi/2, %pi/2, 40)
v = linspace(0, 2*%pi, 20)
x = 5*cos(u)'*cos(v)
y = 10*cos(u)'*sin(v)
z = 1*sin(u)'*ones(v)
plot3d2(x, y, z,flag=[2,4,4])
```

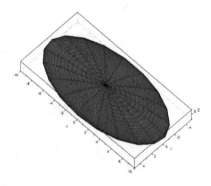

Figure 1.11: Ellipsoid Plot

1.11 Mu_Law

```
function [Cx,Xmax] =mulaw(x,mu) //declaring function mulaw
    using arguments x and mu
Xmax = max(abs(x)) //taking max abs value from all of x
//Applying Mu's Law
if(log(1+mu)~=0)//If mu value is very small
  Cx = (log(1+mu*abs(x/Xmax))./log(1+mu)) // The particular
      entry is calculated with this formula
else //If not
  Cx = x/Xmax //The particular entry is calculated with this
      formula
end//ending if-else
Cx = Cx/Xmax //Dividing all the mu values by Xmax to get the
    final answer
endfunction //ending function, function is now ready to be used
a=input("X values=")// Taking X values
b=input("Mu value=")// Taking Mu value
c=mulaw(a,b) //Applying Mu's law
disp("After Mus Law:")//Displaying text
disp(c)//Displaying result
```

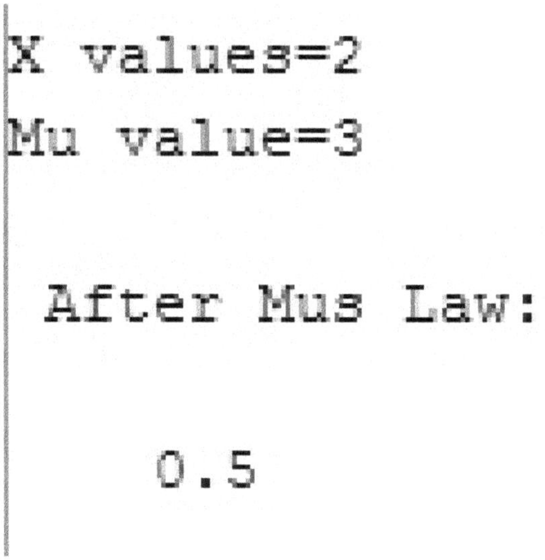

```
X values=2
Mu value=3


After Mus Law:


0.5
```

Figure 1.12: Mu Law

1.12   Parabola

```
a = gca()
a.isoview = 'on'
xc = 0
yc = 0
r = 2
a = linspace(-10, 10, 100);
x = xc + 6*a
y = yc + 3*(a.^2)
plot(x, y)
```

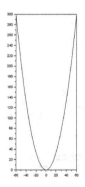

Figure 1.13: Parabola

1.13   Play Sound

```
chdir("D:\007-Muzix\Music")//setting the directory
s1=loadwave('123.wav')//loading first wav file into Scilab
s2=loadwave('234.wav')//loading second wav file into Scilab
subplot(121) // Selecting left hand side for the first graph
xtitle("123.wav") //setting title
analyze(s1) //plotting the wav sound as a graph
subplot(122) // Selecting right hand side for the second graph
xtitle("234.wav") //setting title
analyze(s2) // Plotting the wav sound as a graph
```

1.14   Sphere

```
u = linspace(-%pi/2, %pi/2, 40)
v = linspace(0, 2*%pi, 20)
x = cos(u)'*cos(v)
y = cos(u)'*sin(v)
z = sin(u)'*ones(v)
plot3d2(x, y, z,flag=[2,4,4])
```

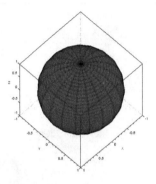

Figure 1.14: Sphere

1.15   Toroid

```
u = linspace(-%pi, %pi, 50) //line space of the first 3D angle
v = linspace(-%pi, %pi, 50) //line space of the second 3D angle
x = (6+3*cos(u)')*cos(v) //x coordinate parametric equation of
    Toroid
y = (6+3*cos(u)')*sin(v) //y coordinate parametric equation of
    Toroid
z = 3*sin(u)'*ones(v) //x coordinate parametric equation of
    Toroid
plot3d2(x, y, z,flag=[2,4,4]) //plotting the 3D graph with
    rectangular planes and using flags to emulate "AxisEqual"
```

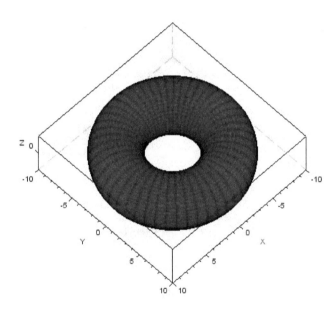

Figure 1.15: Toroid

1.16   Error Correction

```
clear;
clc;
disp("-------------Example 10.13--------------")
function[codeword]=generate_codeword (dataword) // functionto
    generate the codeword at the sender
  r0=bitxor(bitxor(matrix(dataword(4),1,1),matrix(dataword(3)
      ,1,1)),matrix(dataword(2),1,1)); // r0=a0+a1+a2
  s1=bitxor(bitxor(matrix(dataword(3),1,1),matrix(dataword(2)
      ,1,1)),matrix(dataword(1),1,1)); // s1=a1+a2+a3
  r2=bitxor(bitxor(matrix(dataword(3),1,1),matrix(dataword(4)
      ,1,1)),matrix(dataword(1),1,1)); // r2=a0+a1+a3
  codeword=string(dataword(1))+string(dataword(2))+string(
      dataword(3))+string(dataword(4))+string(r2)+string(s1)+
      string(r0); // form the codeword
endfunction
function[syndrome] = generate_syndrome(codeword_recieved) //
    function to generate syndrome at the reciever
  s0=bitxor(bitxor(matrix(codeword_recieved(7),1,1),matrix(
      codeword_recieved(2),1,1)),bitxor(matrix(
      codeword_recieved(3),1,1),matrix(codeword_recieved(4)
      ,1,1))); // s0=b2+b1+b0+q0
  s1=bitxor(bitxor(matrix(codeword_recieved(6),1,1),matrix(
      codeword_recieved(1),1,1)),bitxor(matrix(
      codeword_recieved(2),1,1),matrix(codeword_recieved(3)
      ,1,1))); // s0=b3+b2+b1+q1
  s2=bitxor(bitxor(matrix(codeword_recieved(5),1,1),matrix(
      codeword_recieved(4),1,1)),bitxor(matrix(
      codeword_recieved(3),1,1),matrix(codeword_recieved(1)
      ,1,1))); // s0=b3+b1+b0+q2
  syndrome=string(s2)+string(s1)+string(s0); // the syndrome
      formed
endfunction

function[]=find_error (syndrome,dataword,codeword,
    codeword_recieved) // functin to find the error bit and
    display the final corrected data word
  select syndrome
  case "000"
    dw=string(dataword(1))+string(dataword(2))+string(
        dataword(3))+string(dataword(4));
    cw=string(codeword_recieved(1))+string(codeword_recieved
        (2))+string(codeword_recieved(3))+string(
        codeword_recieved(4))+string(codeword_recieved(5))+
        string(codeword_recieved(6))+string(codeword_recieved
        (7));
    printf("The dataword %s becomes the codeword %s. The
        codeword %s is received.The syndrome is %s (no error),
```

```
        the final dataword is %s.",dw,codeword,cw,syndrome,dw
    );
case "001"
    dw=string(dataword(1))+string(dataword(2))+string(
        dataword(3))+string(dataword(4));
    cw=string(codeword_recieved(1))+string(codeword_recieved
        (2))+string(codeword_recieved(3))+string(
        codeword_recieved(4))+string(codeword_recieved(5))+
        string(codeword_recieved(6))+string(codeword_recieved
        (7));
    error_bit="q0";
    printf("The dataword %s becomes the codeword %s. The
        codeword %s is received. The syndrome is %s.\n%s is
        the error. After flipping %s, the final dataword is %s
        .",dw,codeword,cw,syndrome,error_bit,error_bit,dw);
case "010"
    dw=string(dataword(1))+string(dataword(2))+string(
        dataword(3))+string(dataword(4));
    cw=string(codeword_recieved(1))+string(codeword_recieved
        (2))+string(codeword_recieved(3))+string(
        codeword_recieved(4))+string(codeword_recieved(5))+
        string(codeword_recieved(6))+string(codeword_recieved
        (7));
    error_bit="q1";
    printf("The dataword %s becomes the codeword %s. The
        codeword %s is received. The syndrome is %s.\n%s is
        the error. After flipping %s, the final dataword is %s
        .",dw,codeword,cw,syndrome,error_bit,error_bit,dw);
case "011"
    dw=string(dataword(1))+string(dataword(2))+string(
        dataword(3))+string(dataword(4));
    cw=string(codeword_recieved(1))+string(codeword_recieved
        (2))+string(codeword_recieved(3))+string(
        codeword_recieved(4))+string(codeword_recieved(5))+
        string(codeword_recieved(6))+string(codeword_recieved
        (7));
    error_bit="b2";
    fdw=string(codeword_recieved(1))+string(bitcmp(
        codeword_recieved(2),1))+string(codeword_recieved(3))+
        string(codeword_recieved(4)); // corrected dataword
    printf("The dataword %s becomes the codeword %s. The
        codeword %s is received. The syndrome is %s.\n%s is
        the error. After flipping %s, the final dataword is %s
        .",dw,codeword,cw,syndrome,error_bit,error_bit,fdw);
case "100"
    dw=string(dataword(1))+string(dataword(2))+string(
        dataword(3))+string(dataword(4));
    cw=string(codeword_recieved(1))+string(codeword_recieved
        (2))+string(codeword_recieved(3))+string(
        codeword_recieved(4))+string(codeword_recieved(5))+
```

```
                    string(codeword_recieved(6))+string(codeword_recieved
                    (7));
            error_bit="q2";
            printf("The dataword %s becomes the codeword %s. The
                    codeword %s is received. The syndrome is %s.\n%s is
                    the error. After flipping %s, the final dataword is %s
                    .",dw,codeword,cw,syndrome,error_bit,error_bit,dw);
    case "101"
        dw=string(dataword(1))+string(dataword(2))+string(
                dataword(3))+string(dataword(4));
        cw=string(codeword_recieved(1))+string(codeword_recieved
                (2))+string(codeword_recieved(3))+string(
                codeword_recieved(4))+string(codeword_recieved(5))+
                string(codeword_recieved(6))+string(codeword_recieved
                (7));
        error_bit="b0";
        fdw=string(codeword_recieved(1))+string(codeword_recieved
                (2))+string(codeword_recieved(3))+string(bitcmp(
                codeword_recieved(4),1)); // corrected dataword
        printf("The dataword %s becomes the codeword %s. The
                codeword %s is received. The syndrome is %s.\n%s is
                the error. After flipping %s, the final dataword is %s
                .",dw,codeword,cw,syndrome,error_bit,error_bit,fdw);
    case "110"
        dw=string(dataword(1))+string(dataword(2))+string(
                dataword(3))+string(dataword(4));
        cw=string(codeword_recieved(1))+string(codeword_recieved
                (2))+string(codeword_recieved(3))+string(
                codeword_recieved(4))+string(codeword_recieved(5))+
                string(codeword_recieved(6))+string(codeword_recieved
                (7));
        error_bit="b3";
        fdw=string(bitcmp(codeword_recieved(1),1))+string(
                codeword_recieved(2))+string(codeword_recieved(3))+
                string(codeword_recieved(4)); // corrected dataword
        printf("The dataword %s becomes the codeword %s. The
                codeword %s is received. The syndrome is %s.\n%s is
                the error. After flipping %s, the final dataword is %s
                .",dw,codeword,cw,syndrome,error_bit,error_bit,fdw);
    case "111"
        dw=string(dataword(1))+string(dataword(2))+string(
                dataword(3))+string(dataword(4));
        cw=string(codeword_recieved(1))+string(codeword_recieved
                (2))+string(codeword_recieved(3))+string(
                codeword_recieved(4))+string(codeword_recieved(5))+
                string(codeword_recieved(6))+string(codeword_recieved
                (7));
        error_bit="b1";
        fdw=string(codeword_recieved(1))+string(codeword_recieved
                (2))+string(bitcmp(codeword_recieved(3),1))+string(
```

```
              codeword_recieved(4)); // corrected dataword
        printf("The dataword %s becomes the codeword %s. The
              codeword %s is received. The syndrome is %s.\n%s is
              the error. After flipping %s, the final dataword is %s
              .",dw,codeword,cw,syndrome,error_bit,error_bit,fdw);
    end
endfunction

// 1)
dataword=[0 1 0 0];
codeword=generate_codeword(dataword); // calling the function
codeword_recieved=[0 1 0 0 0 1 1];
syndrome=generate_syndrome(codeword_recieved) // calling the
    function
printf("\n1)");
find_error(syndrome,dataword,codeword,codeword_recieved); //
    calling the function

// 2)
dataword=[0 1 1 1];
codeword=generate_codeword(dataword); // calling the function
codeword_recieved=[0 0 1 1 0 0 1];
syndrome=generate_syndrome(codeword_recieved) // calling the
    function
printf("\n\n2)");
find_error(syndrome,dataword,codeword,codeword_recieved); //
    calling the function

// 3)
dataword=[1 1 0 1];
codeword=generate_codeword(dataword); // calling the function
codeword_recieved=[0 0 0 1 0 0 0];
syndrome=generate_syndrome(codeword_recieved) // calling the
    function
printf("\n\n3)");
find_error(syndrome,dataword,codeword,codeword_recieved); //
    calling the function
printf("\nThis is the wrong dataword. This shows that Hamming
    code cannot correct two errors.");
```

Result

```
1) The dataword 0100 becomes the codeword 0100011. The codeword
   0100011 is received.The syndrome is 000 (no error), the
   final dataword is 0100.
```

2) The dataword 0111 becomes the codeword 0111001. The codeword
   0011001 is received. The syndrome is 011.
b2 is the error. After flipping b2, the final dataword is 0111.

3) The dataword 1101 becomes the codeword 1101000. The codeword
   0001000 is received. The syndrome is 101.
b0 is the error. After flipping b0, the final dataword is 0000.
This is the wrong dataword. This shows that Hamming code cannot
   correct two errors.

1.17   Hamming Distance

```
clear;
clc;
disp("Hamming Distance")
//words
x1=[0 0 0];
y1=[0 1 1];
x2=[1 0 1 0 1];
y2=[1 1 1 1 0];
// formula to find Hamming distance 'd'
distance1=bitxor(x1,y1);
distance2=bitxor(x2,y2);
function [count]= num_of_ones (distance)// function to find the
    number of ones in a binary number
   count=0;
   for i=1:length(distance)
     if(distance(i)== 1)
         count = count+1; // number of one's
     end
   end
endfunction
distance=num_of_ones(distance1); // calling the function
printf("\nThe Hamming distance distance(OOO, 011) is %d.\n",
    distance); // display result
distance=num_of_ones(distance2); // calling the function
printf("\nThe Hamming distance distance(10101, 11110) is %d.\n"
    ,distance); // display result
```

Result

```
 Hamming Distance

The Hamming distance distance(OOO, 011) is 2.

The Hamming distance distance(10101, 11110) is 3.
```

1.18   Minimum Hamming Distance

```
clear;
clc;
disp("--------------Example 10.6--------------")
//words
x1=[0 0 0 0 0];
x2=[0 1 0 1 1];
x3=[1 0 1 0 1];
x4=[1 1 1 1 0];
//function to find Hamming distance
function [d]=hamming_distance(x,y)
   xd=bitxor(x,y);
   d=num_of_ones(xd);
endfunction
function [count]= num_of_ones (d)// function to find the number
    of ones in a binary number
   count=0;
   for i=1:length(d)
     if(d(i)== 1)
         count = count+1;  //number of ones
       end
    end
endfunction
d1=hamming_distance(x1,x2);
printf("\nThe Hamming distance d(00000, 01011) is %d.\n",d1);
    // display result
d2=hamming_distance(x1,x3);
printf("\nThe Hamming distance d(00000, 10101) is %d.\n",d2);
    // display result
d3=hamming_distance(x1,x4);
printf("\nThe Hamming distance d(00000, 11110) is %d.\n",d3);
    // display result
d4=hamming_distance(x2,x3);
printf("\nThe Hamming distance d(01011, 10101) is %d.\n",d4);
    // display result
d5=hamming_distance(x2,x4);
printf("\nThe Hamming distance d(01011, 11110) is %d.\n",d5);
    // display result
d6=hamming_distance(x3,x4);
printf("\nThe Hamming distance d(10101, 11110) is %d.\n",d6);
    // display result
dmin=min(d1,d2,d3,d4,d5,d6);
printf("\nThe minimum Hamming distance dmin is %d.",dmin); //
    display result
```

Result

```
The Hamming distance d(OOOOO, 01011) is 3.

The Hamming distance d(OOOOO, 10101) is 3.

The Hamming distance d(OOOOO, 11110) is 4.

The Hamming distance d(O1011, 10101) is 4.

The Hamming distance d(O1011, 11110) is 3.

The Hamming distance d(10101, 11110) is 3.

The minimum Hamming distance dmin is 3.
```

1.19 3D Spline Interpolation

```
exec("SCI/modules/interpolation/demos/interp_demo.sci")
func = "v=(x-0.5).^2 + (y-0.5).^3 + (z-0.5).^2";
deff("v=f(x,y,z)",func);
n = 5;
x = linspace(0,1,n); y=x; z=x;
[X,Y,Z] = ndgrid(x,y,z);
V = f(X,Y,Z);
tl = splin3d(x,y,z,V);
// compute (and display) the 3d spline interpolant on some
    slices
m = 41;
direction = ["z=" "z=" "z=" "x=" "y="];
val = [ 0.1 0.5 0.9 0.5 0.5];
ebox = [0 1 0 1 0 1];
XF=[]; YF=[]; ZF=[]; VF=[];
for i = 1:length(val)
  [Xm,Xp,Ym,Yp,Zm,Zp] = slice_parallelepiped(direction(i), val(i
      ), ebox, m, m, m);
  Vm = interp3d(Xm,Ym,Zm, tl);
  [xf,yf,zf,vf] = nf3dq(Xm,Ym,Zm,Vm,1);
  XF = [XF xf]; YF = [YF yf]; ZF = [ZF zf]; VF = [VF vf];
  Vp = interp3d(Xp,Yp,Zp, tl);
  [xf,yf,zf,vf] = nf3dq(Xp,Yp,Zp,Vp,1);
  XF = [XF xf]; YF = [YF yf]; ZF = [ZF zf]; VF = [VF vf];
end
nb_col = 128;
vmin = min(VF); vmax = max(VF);
color_example = dsearch(VF,linspace(vmin,vmax,nb_col+1));
xset("colormap",jetcolormap(nb_col));
clf(); xset("hidden3d",xget("background"));
colorbar(vmin,vmax)
plot3d(XF, YF, list(ZF,color_example), flag=[-1 6 4])
xtitle("3d spline interpolation of "+func)
show_window()
```

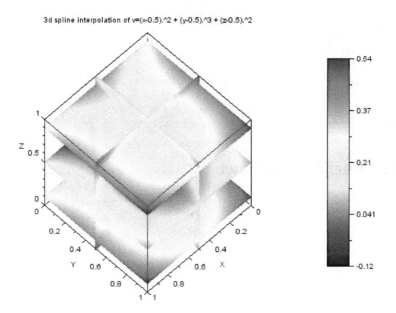

Figure 1.16: 3D Spline

1.20   ASCII Value Printing

```
ascii([98 121 101])
ascii("My Name is Ankit Dua")
```

1.21   Dijikstra Network Topology

```
n=100;
L=1500;
dmax=100;
[g]NtgLocaltyConnex(n,L,dmax);
i=Random(length(g.node x);
show_graph(g);
hilite_nodes(i);
[dist,pred]=MobilityDijkstra(g.node_x);
i
dist
```

1.22   Euclidian Distance

```
n=50;
L=500;
dmax=120;
[g]=NtgLocalityConnex(n,L,dmax);
N=length(g.node_x);
[n1,n2]=Random_i_j(N);
nd=ones(1,n);
nc=ones(1,n);
nd([n1 n2])=3;
nc([n1 n2])=5;
g.node_border=nd;
g.node_color=nc;
show_graph(g);
[d]=Distance(n1,n2,g.node_x,g.node_y);
n1
n2
```

1.23   Extract Largest Connex

```
n=100;
```

```
L=200;
dmax=50;
[g]=NtgLocality(n,L,dmax);
[g1]=GraphConnex(g);
show_graph(g);
show_graph(g1);
```

1.24 Generating Random Integers

```
n=100;
nd=1;
[nf]=AleaInitFin(n,nd);
[n:nd:nf]
```

1.25 Plot 3D

```
function z = f(x,y)
   z = 2*x^2+y^2;
endfunction
x = linspace(-1,1,100);
y = linspace(-2,2,200);
z = feval(x,y,f)';
clf
surf(x,y,z)
```

1.26   Discrete Calculation

```
v=(1:8)^3;
diff(v)
diff(v,3)

A=[(1:8)^2
  (1:8)^3
  (1:8)^4];

diff(A,3,2)

//approximate differentiation
step=0.001
t=0:step:10;
y=sin(t);
dy=diff(sin(t))/step; //approximate differentiation of sine
    function
norm(dy-cos(t(1:$-1)),%inf)
```

1.27   Topology Generation

```
n=80;//network size
L=1000;//network square area side
dmax=100;//locality radius
[g]=NtgLocalityConnex(n,L,dmax);//generation of a random
    topology in respect with the Locality method.
i=Random(length(g.node_x));//selection of the source node
show_graph(g);
hilite_nodes(i);
[dist,pred]=MobilityDijkstra(g.node_x,g.node_y,g.head,g.tail,i)
    ;//Application of MobilityDijkstra
i
dist
pred
```

Sample 2

```
n=80;//network size
L=1000;//network square area side
dmax=100;//locality radius
[g]=NtgLocalityConnex(n,L,dmax);//generation of a random
    topology in respect with the Locality method.
i=Random(length(g.node_x));//selection of the source node
show_graph(g);
hilite_nodes(i);
```

```
[dist,pred]=MobilityDijkstra(g.node_x,g.node_y,g.head,g.tail,i)
    ;//Application of MobilityDijkstra
i
dist
pred
```

Sample 3

```
n=80;//network size
L=1000;//network square area side
dmax=100;//locality radius
[g]=NtgLocalityConnex(n,L,dmax);//generation of a random
    topology in respect with the Locality method.
i=Random(length(g.node_x));//selection of the source node
show_graph(g);
hilite_nodes(i);
[dist,pred]=MobilityDijkstra(g.node_x,g.node_y,g.head,g.tail,i)
    ;//Application of MobilityDijkstra
i
dist
pred
```

1.28   New Node Central

```
n=150
L=1000
dmax=100
[g]=NtgLocalityConnex(n,L,dmax)
gn=length(g.node_x)
i=Random(gn))
N=20
d=50
[ge]=CirclePlace(N,d,g,i)
ge.edge_color=[ones(1,length(g.head)) 5*ones(1,N)]
ge.edge_width=[ones(1,length(g.head)) 1.5*ones(1,N)]
ge.node_color=[ones(1,length(g.node_x)) 5*ones(1,N)]
ge.node_border=[ones(1,length(g.node_x)) 1.5*ones(1,N)]
show_graph(ge)
```

1.29   Plot Sin and Cos

```
N = 100;
n = 0:N - 1;
w1 = %pi/5;
w2 = %pi/10;
s1 = cos(w1*n);
s2 = cos(w2*n);
f = s1 + s2;
F = fft(f);
F_abs = abs(F);
plot(n, F_abs);
```

1.30   Finding Largest Eigen Value Matrix

```
//finding largest Eigen value of given matrix
clear;
clc;
close();
A=[3 0 1;2 2 2;4 2 5];
u0=[1 1 1]';
v=A*u0;
a=max(u0);
while abs(max(v)-a)>0.05
  a=max(v);
  u0=v/max(v);
  v=A*u0;
end
format('v',4);
disp(max(v),'Eigen value :')
format('v',5);
disp(u0,'Eigen vector :')
```

1.31   Euler's Method For Solving IVP

```
//Euler's Method For Solving IVP
clc;
clear;
close();
format('v',8);
funcprot(0);
```

```
deff('[g]=f(x,y)','g= -y^2/(1+x)');
y = 1;
x = 0;
h = 0.05;
while x<0.2
    y = y - 0.05*y^2/(1+x);
    x = x + h;
    disp(y,x,'Value of y at x :');
end
disp(y,'The calculated value of y(0.2):');
x = 0.2;
act = 1/(1+log(1+x));
disp(act,'The exact value is of y(0.2): ');
err = act - y;
disp(err,'The error is :');
```

1.32 Integration Calculation

```
clc;
clear;
close();
format('v',8);
funcprot(0);
disp('Integral 0 to 2 exp(x)dx');
deff('[t]=f(x,y)','t=-y^2/(1+x)');
yn = 1;
xn = 0;
h = 0.05;
for i = 1:4
    k1 = f(xn,yn);
    k2 = f(xn+0.5*h,yn+.5*h*k1);
    k3 = f(xn+0.5*h,yn+.5*h*k2);
    k4 = f(xn+h,yn+h*k3);
    yn_1 = yn + h*(k1+2*k2+2*k3+k4)/6;
    n = i-1;
    ann(:,i) = [n k1 k2 k3 k4 yn_1]';
    yn = yn_1;
    xn = xn+h;
end
disp(ann,'Calculated integration : ');
```

1.33 Finding lowest and upper matrices

```
// to find L and U matrices
clear;
close();
clc;
format('v',5);
A = {4,-2,2;4,-3,-2;2,3,-1];
L(1,1)=1;L(2,2)=1;L(3,3)=1;
for i=1:3
  for j=1:3
    s=0;
    if j>=i
      for k=1:i-1
        s=s+L(i,k)*U(k,j);
      end
      U(i,j)=A(i,j)-s;
    else
      for k=1:j-1
        s=s+L(i,k)*U(k,j);
      end
      L(i,j)=(A(i,j)-s)/U(j,j);
    end
  end
end
disp(L,'L =')
disp(U,'U =')
```

1.34   Number of iteration matrix value

```
clear;
close();
clc;
format('v',7);
x1=[0,0];
x2=[0,0];
x3=[0,0];
x1(1,2)=0.2*(6-2*x2(1,1)+x3(1,1));
x2(1,2)=0.16667*(4-x1(1,2)+3*x3(1,1));
x3(1,2)=0.25*(7-2*x1(1,2)-x2(1,2));
i=1;
while (abs(x1(1,1)-x1(1,2))>0.5*10^-2 | abs(x2(1,1)-x2(1,2))
    >0.5*10^-2 | abs(x3(1,1)-x3(1,2))>0.5*10^-2 )
  x1(1,1)=x1(1,2);
  x2(1,1)=x2(1,2);
  x3(1,1)=x3(1,2);
  x1(1,2)=0.2*(6-2*x2(1,1)+x3(1,1));
  x2(1,2)=0.16667*(4-x1(1,2)+3*x3(1,1));
  x3(1,2)=0.25*(7-2*x1(1,2)-x2(1,2));
```

```
    i=i+1;
end
disp([x1; x2; x3],'Answers are :')
disp(i,'Number of Iterations :')
```

1.35 Positive Root of the function

```
clc;
clear;
close();
funcprot(0);
format('v',9);
deff('[Newton]=fx(x)','Newton=exp(x)-x-2');
deff('[diff]=gx(x)','diff=exp(x)-1');
x = linspace(-2.5,1.5);
plot(x,exp(x)-x-2)
//from the graph the function has 2 roots
//considering the initial negative root -10
x1 = -10;
x2 = x1-fx(x1)/gx(x1);
i=0;
while abs(x1-x2)>(0.5*10^-7)
    x1=x2;
    x2 = x1-fx(x1)/gx(x1);
    i=i+1;
end
disp(i,'Number of iterations : ')
disp(x2,'The negative root of the function is : ')


//considering the initial positive root 10
x1 = 10;
x2 = x1-fx(x1)/gx(x1);
i=0;
while abs(x1-x2)>(0.5*10^-7)
    x1=x2;
    x2 = x1-fx(x1)/gx(x1);
    i=i+1;
end
disp(i,'Number of iteration : ')
disp(x2,'The positive root of the function is : ')
```

1.36   RED and GREEN Matrix of Image

```
a= imread('C:\Users\Vishnu\Pictures\IMG_1356.jpg');
figure
ar=a(:,:,1);
ShowImage(ar,'RED Matrix')
figure
ag=a(:,:,2);
ShowImage(ag,'GREEN Matrix')
```

1.37   Prime number checking

```
x=input("Enter any number ");
flag=0;

for i = 2:(x-1)
 if(modulo(x,i)==0) then
 flag=1;
 break;
 end;
end

if(flag==1) then
 disp("not prime number");
else
 disp("prime number");
end;
```

1.38   Coloring Image

```
xdel(winsid());
clear;
clc;
x = linspace(-5,5,51);
y = 1 ./(1+x.^2);
scf(1);
clf(1);
plot(x,y,'o-b');
xlabel("$-5\le x\le 5$","fontsize",4,"color","red");
ylabel("$y(x)=\frac{1}{1+x^2}$","fontsize",4,"color","red");
title("Runge function (#Points =
"+string(length(x))+").","color","red","fontsize",4);
legend("Function evaluation");
```

1.39   Dynamic Equation

```
xdel(winsid());
clear;
clc;
function y=u(t)
    y=(sign(t)+1)/2
endfunction

L=0.001
R=10
C=0.000001

function zdot=f(t,y)
    zdot(1)= y(2);
    zdot(2)=(u(t)-y(1)-L*y(2)/R)/(L*C);
endfunction

y0=[0,0];
t0=0;
t=0:0.00001:0.001;
out=ode(y0,t0,t,f);
clf();
plot(out);
```

1.40   Diagonalisation

```
xdel(winsid());
clear;
clc;

a=[1 2 3;4 5 6 ;7 8 9]
b=[9 1 3;12 3 5;9 3 1]
c=a+b
d=spec(a)
[D,V]=bdiag(c)
[V,D] = spec(c)
[al,be] = spec(a,b); d = al./be;
d = spec(a,b)
d = spec(inv(b)*a)
[al,be,V] = spec(a,b); D = diag(al./be);
```

1.41   Inverse Laplace Transform Partial Difference

```
xdel(winsid());
clear;
clc;
s=%s
num=s^5+8*s^4+23*s^3+35*s^2+28*s+3;
den=s^3+6*s^2+8*s;
g=syslin('c',num/den);
gf=tf2ss(g);
se=pfss(gf);
for k=1:size(se),
df(k)=clean(se[k]);
end;
```

1.42 Laplace Transform Partial Difference Calculation

```
xdel(winsid());
clear;
clc;
s=%s;
num=2*s^3+5*s^2+3*s+6;
den=s^3+6*s^2+11*s+6;
g=syslin('c',num/den);
gf=tf2ss(g);
se=pfss(gf);
```

1.43 Subplot

```
xdel(winsid());
clear;
clc;
t=[0:0.1:4*%pi]';
subplot(221)
plot(t,[sin(t) sin(2*t) sin(3*t)]);
xtitle("sin(t),sin(2t),sin(3t) versus t")
subplot(222)
plot(t,cos(t)')
xtitle("cos(t) versus t")
subplot(223)
plot(t,t.^2)
xtitle("t^2 versus t")
subplot(224)
plot(t,sqrt(t))
xtitle("sqrt(t) versus t")
```

1.44 Bubble Sort

```
disp("enter the no. of variables")
n=input('')
disp("enter the no.")
for i=1:n
x(i)=input('');
end
for i=1:n
for j=1:n-i-1
if x(j) > x(j+1) then
temp=x(j)
x(j)=x(j+1)
x(j+1)=temp
end
end
end
for i=1:n
disp(x(i))
end
```

1.45 Insertion Sort

```
disp("enter the no. of variables")
n=input('')
disp("enter the no.")
for i=1:n
x(i)=input('');
end
for i=2:n
for j=i:-1:2
if x(j) < x(j-1) then
temp=x(j);
x(j)=x(j-1);
x(j-1)=temp;
end
end
end
disp("sorted list is")
for i=1:n
disp(x(i))
end
```

1.46 Selection Sort

```
disp("enter the no. of variables")
n=input('')
disp("enter the no.")
for i=1:n
x(i)=input('');
end
for i=1:n-1
posmin=i
for j=i+1:n
if x(j)<x(posmin)
posmin=j
end
end
if posmin~=i then
temp=x(i)
x(i)=x(posmin)
x(posmin)=temp
end
end
for i=1:n
disp(x(i))
end
```

1.47   Armstrong Number

```
clear, clc
for i = 100 : 999
is = num2str(i);
i1 = str2num(is(1));
i2 = str2num(is(2));
disp([i an])
end
end
```

1.48   Bisection

```
funcprot(0)

function [p]=Bisection (a,b,f,Tol)
   N=100; // Maximum number of iterations
   if(f(a)*f(b)>0) then
      error('Root does not exist f(a)*f(b)>0')
      abort;
   end
   mprintf("Iterations a b f(c)\n")
   mprintf("                          \n")

   while(N>0)
      c=(a+b)/2;
      if (abs(f(c))< Tol)then //Stopping Criteria
         p=c;

         return ;
      end

      if(f(a)*f(c)<0) then
         b=c;
      else
         a=c;
      end

endfunction
```

1.49   Gauss Jordan Elimination

```
format('e',20)
```

```
A=input("Enter the coefficient matrix: ")
b=input("Enter the right-hand side matrix: ")
function[x]=GaussJordanElimination(A,b)

    //This function solves the system Ax=B by using Gauss Jordan
        Elimination
//Retrive the size of A and size of b are compatible

                    if( m<>r)then
                        error("Error: matrix A and vector B are
                            incompatible sizes");
                    end

// Create the augmented system C
                C=[A b]

//Dimension of the augmented system C are [m, n]
            [m,n]= size(C)

//Compute the Gauss-Jordan elimination
//Loop over the rows for pivoting.Let this index k,
// we are "pivoting" column k, that the pivot is at index
//C(k.k) and we want zeros below and above C(k,k) in column k.

for k=1:1:m
    indices= [ 1 : 1 : k-1, k+1 : 1 : m ]

//For all rows below and above the pivot, subtract a multiple
// of the pivoting row to get a zero
            for i= indices
                multiplier= C(i,k)/C(k,k)
                for j= k+1:n
                    C(i,j)=C(i,j)-multiplier*C(k,j)
                end
            end
        end
        print(6,C)

// Create a zero solution
        x=zeros( m,s )

//Solve for all the s right-hand sides
        for i=1 : 1: m
            for i=1: 1: s
                x(i,j)=C(i, m+j)/C(i,i)
            end
        end
        return x
    endfunction
```

1.50   Naive Gaussian Elimination

```
format('e',20)
funcprot(0)
A=input("Enter the coefficient matrix of nXn: ")
B=input("Enter the right-hand side matrix nX1:")

    function[x]= naivegaussianelimination(A,B)

//This function obtains the solutions to the systems of linear
    equations
//A*X=, given the matrix coefficients A nad the right-hand side
    vector,B
//Gaussian elimaination
//Inputs:
//A- matrix of real numbers of size nXn
//B-matrix of real numbers of size nX1
//X-the solution to the given equation

//Retrive the size of matrix A and vector B
        [n,n1]=size(A);
        [m1,p]=size(B);

//Check that size of A and size of B are compatible
if n~=n1 then
    error('gaussianelimination- Matrix A must be square');
    abort;
else if n~=m1
        error('gaussianelimination- incompatible dimension of A &
            B');
        abort;

end;

//Create the augmented system C
        C=[A B];

//Forward Elimination
        n=size(A,1);
        for k=1:n-1
            for i=k+1:n
                factor=A(i,k)/A(k,k);
                    for j=k+1:n
                        A(i,j)=A(i,j)-factor*A(k,j);
                    end
```

```
                B(i)=B(i)-factor*B(k);
            end
            end
        end
//Back Substitution
        x(n)=B(n)/A(n,n);
        for i=n-1:-1:1
            sum=0;
            for j=i+1:n
                sum=sum+A(i,j)*x(j);
            end
            x(i)=(B(i)-sum)/A(i,i);
        end
    endfunction
```

1.51 Calculator

```
mode(7)

0.4 + 4/2
0.4 + 4/2
ans/2
(0.4 + 4)/(3-4^0.5)
1*2 , 1.1 + 1.3
1 + 1/2 + 1/3 + ...
1/4 + 1/5 + ...
1/6
1 + 1/2 + 1/3 + 1/4 + 1/5 + 1/6;
ans


%pi
sin(%pi)
%i
sqrt(-1)
exp(%i*%pi)+1
ieee(2)
1/0
0/0, %inf*%inf, %inf*%nan
ieee(0)
format('v',20); %pi
format('e',20); %pi
format("v",10); %pi
a = 4/3;
b = 3/4;
c = a*b;
disp(c)
a = 'Hello';
b = 'World';
// String concatenation
c = a + " " + b + "!" ;
disp(c);
// Concatenation of a string with a number
d = "Length of " + a + " is " + string(length(a))
// Example of a true expression (boolean)
res = 1>0
// Example of a false expression (boolean)
res = 1<0
// a contains a number
a = 1;
disp(a)
// a is now a string
a = 'Hello!';
```

```
disp(a)

// FUNCTIONS
rand
sin(%pi)
max(1,2)
max(1,2,5,4,2)
// Examples of output arguments
a = rand()
v = max(1,2,5,4,2)
[v,k] = max(1,2,5,4,2)

// RESOLUTION OF A QUADRATIC EQUATION
// Define input data
a = 3; b = -2; c = -1/3;
// Compute delta
Delta = b^2-4*a*c;
// Compute solutions
x1 = (-b+sqrt(Delta))/(2*a);
x2 = (-b-sqrt(Delta))/(2*a);
// Display the solutions
disp(x1); disp(x2);
// Exact solutions
x1e = (1+sqrt(2))/3
x2e = (1-sqrt(2))/3
// Compute differences between solutions
diff_x1 = abs(x1-x1e)
diff_x2 = abs(x2-x2e)
```

Output

```
-->

-->mode(7)
Pause mode: enter empty lines to continue.

>>
>>0.4 + 4/2
 ans =

   2.4
>>0.4 + 4/2
>>ans/2
 ans =

   1.2
>>(0.4 + 4)/(3-4^0.5)
```

```
>>1*2 , 1.1 + 1.3
 ans =

   2.
 ans =

   2.4
>>1 + 1/2 + 1/3 + ...
>>1/4 + 1/5 + ...
>>1/6
 ans =

   0.6166667
>>1 + 1/2 + 1/3 + 1/4 + 1/5 + 1/6;
>>ans
 ans =

   0.6166667
>>
>>
>>%pi
>>sin(%pi)
 ans =

   1.225D-16
>>%i
>>sqrt(-1)
 ans =

   i
>>exp(%i*%pi)+1
>>ieee(2)
>>1/0
>>0/0, %inf*%inf, %inf*%nan
 ans =

   Nan
 ans =

   Inf
 ans =

   Nan
>>ieee(0)
>>format('v',20); %pi
 %pi =

   3.14159265358979312
>>format('e',20); %pi
>>format("v",10); %pi
```

```
 %pi  =

    3.1415927
>>a = 4/3;
>>b = 3/4;
>>c = a*b;
>>disp(c)

  - 0.3333333
>>a = 'Hello';
>>b = 'World';
>>// String concatenation
>>c = a + " " + b + "!" ;
        !--error 144
Undefined operation for the given operands.
check or define function %s_a_c for overloading.


-->disp(c);

  - 0.3333333

-->// Concatenation of a string with a number

-->d = "Length of " + a + " is " + string(length(a))
                !--error 144
Undefined operation for the given operands.
check or define function %c_a_s for overloading.


-->// Example of a true expression (boolean)

-->res = 1>0
 res =

  T

-->// Example of a false expression (boolean)

-->res = 1<0
 res =

  F

-->// a contains a number

-->a = 1;

-->disp(a)
```

```
    1.

-->// a is now a string

-->a = 'Hello!';

-->disp(a)

 Hello!

-->

-->// FUNCTIONS

-->rand
 ans =

    0.0002211

-->sin(%pi)
 ans =

    1.225D-16

-->max(1,2)
 ans =

    2.

-->max(1,2,5,4,2)
 ans =

    5.

-->// Examples of output arguments

-->a = rand()
 a =

    0.3303271

-->v = max(1,2,5,4,2)
 v =

    5.

-->[v,k] = max(1,2,5,4,2)
 k =

    3.
```

```
 v =

    5.

-->

-->// RESOLUTION OF A QUADRATIC EQUATION

-->// Define input data

-->a = 3; b = -2; c = -1/3;

-->// Compute delta

-->Delta = b^2-4*a*c;

-->// Compute solutions

-->x1 = (-b+sqrt(Delta))/(2*a);

-->x2 = (-b-sqrt(Delta))/(2*a);

-->// Display the solutions

-->disp(x1); disp(x2);

    0.8047379

  - 0.1380712

-->// Exact solutions

-->x1e = (1+sqrt(2))/3
 x1e =

    0.8047379

-->x2e = (1-sqrt(2))/3
 x2e =

  - 0.1380712

-->// Compute differences between solutions

-->diff_x1 = abs(x1-x1e)
 diff_x1 =

    0.

-->diff_x2 = abs(x2-x2e)
```

```
diff_x2 =

   0.

-->
```

1.52   Hamming distance

```
clear;
clc;
disp("Hamming Distance")
//words
x1=[0 0 0];
y1=[0 1 1];
x2=[1 0 1 0 1];
y2=[1 1 1 1 0];
// formula to find Hamming distance 'd'
d1=bitxor(x1,y1);
d2=bitxor(x2,y2);
function [count]= num_of_ones (d)// function to find the number
    of ones in a binary number
  count=0;
  for i=1:length(d)
    if(d(i)== 1)
        count = count+1; // number of one's
    end
  end
endfunction
d=num_of_ones(d1); // calling the function
printf("\nThe Hamming distance d(OOO, 011) is %d.\n",d); //
   display result
d=num_of_ones(d2); // calling the function
printf("\nThe Hamming distance d(10101, 11110) is %d.\n",d); //
    display result
```

1.53   Heart Shaped Curve

```
Scilab 5.5.2 (Mar 31 2015, 12:04:21)

-->x1=linspace(-1,0,50)
 x1 =

        column 1 to 6

 - 1. - 0.9795918 - 0.9591837 - 0.9387755 - 0.9183673 -
    0.8979592

        column 7 to 12

 - 0.8775510 - 0.8571429 - 0.8367347 - 0.8163265 - 0.7959184 -
    0.7755102

        column 13 to 18

 - 0.7551020 - 0.7346939 - 0.7142857 - 0.6938776 - 0.6734694 -
    0.6530612

        column 19 to 24

 - 0.6326531 - 0.6122449 - 0.5918367 - 0.5714286 - 0.5510204 -
    0.5306122

        column 25 to 30

 - 0.5102041 - 0.4897959 - 0.4693878 - 0.4489796 - 0.4285714 -
    0.4081633

        column 31 to 36

 - 0.3877551 - 0.3673469 - 0.3469388 - 0.3265306 - 0.3061224 -
    0.2857143

        column 37 to 42

 - 0.2653061 - 0.2448980 - 0.2244898 - 0.2040816 - 0.1836735 -
    0.1632653

        column 43 to 48

 - 0.1428571 - 0.1224490 - 0.1020408 - 0.0816327 - 0.0612245 -
    0.0408163

        column 49 to 50
```

```
  - 0.0204082 0.

-->y1=-x1+sqrt(3-3*x1.^2);

-->y2=-x1-sqrt(3-3*x1.^2);

-->title('Heart Shape Curve');

-->plot(x1,y1,'r');

-->plot(-x1,y1,'r');

-->plot(-x1,y2,'r');

-->plot(x1,y2,'r');

-->
```

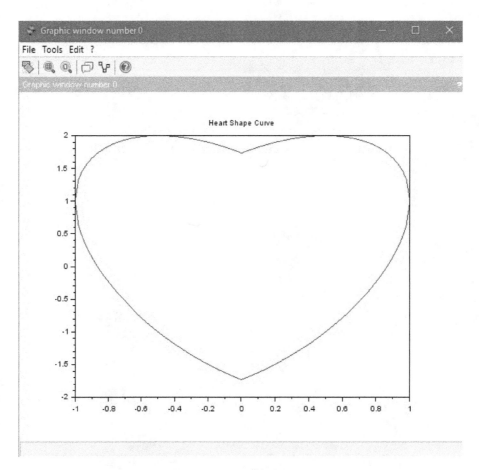

Figure 1.17: Heart Shaped Curve

Chapter 2

Network Topologies Creation and Routing using Scilab

2.1 BFS to a random source node and display the corresponding graphs

```
//This graph is to apply BFS to a random source node and
    display the corresponding graphs.

//generation of plot using 10 nodes
//1.generation of topology in barabasi alebert using BFS plot
//2.generation of edge number.
//3.generation of BFS plot

NumberOfNodes=10;//number of nodes
links=3;//a maximum of 3 links are created for any created node
area=1000;//network square area side
localityradius=100;//Locality radius
[TopologyGraph]=NL_T_LocalityConnex(NumberOfNodes,area,
    localityradius);//generation of a topology in respect with
    the Locality method
display=5;//display parameter
WindowNumber=1;//window index
//1. generation of topology in barabasi alebert using BFS plot

[TopologyGraph,NodeDiameter]=NL_T_BarabasiAlbert(NumberOfNodes,
    links,area);//application of NL_T_BarabasiAlbert
//xtitle("generation of topology in barabasi alebert using BFS
    plot for 10 nodes","X-Nodes","Y-Nodes");
//2.generation of edge number
```

```
VisualizeNodesEdges=NL_G_ShowGraphE(TopologyGraph,WindowNumber)
    ;// to show the graph
xtitle("generation of edge number for 10 nodes.","X-Nodes","Y-
    Nodes");
[l]=NL_G_EdgeNumber(TopologyGraph)//application of
    NL_G_EdgeNumber
WindowNumber=2;//window index
VisualizeNodesEdges=NL_G_ShowGraphN(TopologyGraph,WindowNumber)
    ;//graph visualization
xtitle("generation of BFS plot for 10 nodes","X-Nodes","Y-Nodes
    ");
i=NL_F_RandInt1n(length(TopologyGraph.node_x));//selection of
    the source node
display=5;//display parameter
WindowNumber=3;//window index
//3.generation of BFS plot

[go,v,pred]=NL_R_BFSPlot(TopologyGraph,i,display,WindowNumber);
    //application of NL_R_BFSPlot
i
v(1:10)//first ten values
pred(1:10)//first ten values
disp(go,v,pred);// to display the values in console


//generation of plot using 50 nodes
//1.generation of topology in barabasi alebert using BFS plot
//2.generation of edge number.
//3.generation of BFS plot

NumberOfNodes=50;//number of nodes
links=3;//a maximum of 3 links are created for any created node
area=1000;//network square area side
localityradius=100;//Locality radius
[TopologyGraph]=NL_T_LocalityConnex(NumberOfNodes,area,
    localityradius);//generation of a topology in respect with
    the Locality method
display=5;//display parameter
WindowNumber=4;//window index
//1. generation of topology in barabasi alebert using BFS plot

[TopologyGraph,NodeDiameter]=NL_T_BarabasiAlbert(NumberOfNodes,
    links,area);//application of NL_T_BarabasiAlbert
xtitle("generation of topology in barabasi alebert using BFS
    plot for 50 nodes","X-Nodes","Y-Nodes");
//2.generation of edge number

VisualizeNodesEdges=NL_G_ShowGraphE(TopologyGraph,WindowNumber)
    ;// to show the graph
```

```
xtitle("generation of edge number for 50 nodes.","X-Nodes","Y-
    Nodes");
[l]=NL_G_EdgeNumber(TopologyGraph)//application of
    NL_G_EdgeNumber
WindowNumber=5;//window index
VisualizeNodesEdges=NL_G_ShowGraphN(TopologyGraph,WindowNumber)
    ;//graph visualization
xtitle("generation of BFS plot for 50 nodes","X-Nodes","Y-Nodes
    ");
i=NL_F_RandInt1n(length(TopologyGraph.node_x));//selection of
    the source node
display=5;//display parameter
WindowNumber=6;//window index
//3.generation of BFS plot


[go,v,pred]=NL_R_BFSPlot(TopologyGraph,i,display,WindowNumber);
    //application of NL_R_BFSPlot
i
v(1:10)//first ten values
pred(1:10)//first ten values
disp(go,v,pred);// to display the values in console



//generation of plot using 100 nodes
//1.generation of topology in barabasi alebert using BFS plot
//2.generation of edge number.
//3.generation of BFS plot

NumberOfNodes=100;//number of nodes
links=3;//a maximum of 3 links are created for any created node
area=1000;//network square area side
localityradius=100;//Locality radius
[TopologyGraph]=NL_T_LocalityConnex(NumberOfNodes,area,
    localityradius);//generation of a topology in respect with
    the Locality method
display=5;//display parameter
WindowNumber=7;//window index
//1. generation of topology in barabasi alebert using BFS plot

[TopologyGraph,NodeDiameter]=NL_T_BarabasiAlbert(NumberOfNodes,
    links,area);//application of NL_T_BarabasiAlbert
xtitle("generation of topology in barabasi alebert using BFS
    plot for 100 nodes","X-Nodes","Y-Nodes");
//2.generation of edge number

VisualizeNodesEdges=NL_G_ShowGraphE(TopologyGraph,WindowNumber)
    ;// to show the graph
xtitle("generation of edge number for 100 nodes.","X-Nodes","Y-
    Nodes");
```

```
[l]=NL_G_EdgeNumber(TopologyGraph)//application of
    NL_G_EdgeNumber
WindowNumber=8;//window index
VisualizeNodesEdges=NL_G_ShowGraphN(TopologyGraph,WindowNumber)
    ;//graph visualization
xtitle("generation of BFS plot for 100 nodes","X-Nodes","Y-
    Nodes");
i=NL_F_RandInt1n(length(TopologyGraph.node_x));//selection of
    the source node
display=5;//display parameter
WindowNumber=9;//window index
//3.generation of BFS plot

[go,v,pred]=NL_R_BFSPlot(TopologyGraph,i,display,WindowNumber);
    //application of NL_R_BFSPlot
i
v(1:10)//first ten values
pred(1:10)//first ten values
disp(go,v,pred);// to display the values in console
```

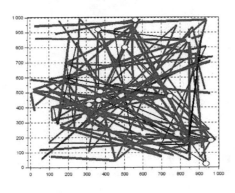
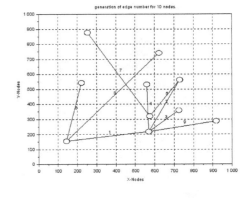
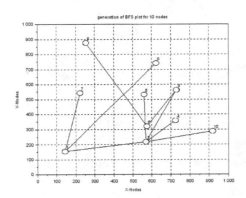
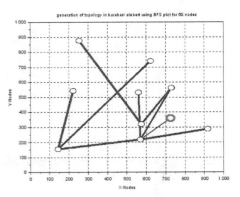

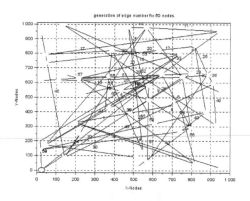

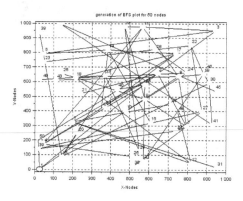

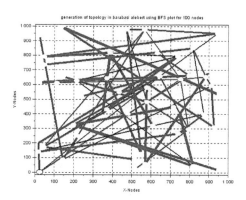

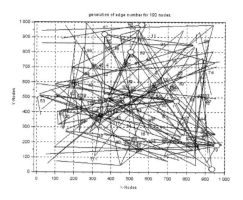

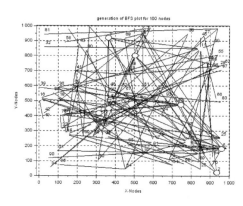

2.2   Topology Creation For BFS

```
//This graph is to apply BFS to a random source node and
    display the corresponding graphs.
//generation of graph using 5 lines and 5 columns
//1. generation of topology in Grid using BFS plot.
//2. generation of BFS plot.
lines=5;//number of lines
columns=5;//number of columns
links=5;// maximum of 5 links are created for any created node
x_area=1000;//network area x-side
y_area=1000;//network area x-side
//1.generation of topology in Grid using BFS plot.
display=10;//display parameter
WindowNumber=1;//window index
[TopologyGraph]=NL_T_Grid(lines,columns,x_area,y_area);//
    application of NL_T_Grid
VisualizeNodesEdges=NL_G_ShowGraphNE(TopologyGraph,WindowNumber
    );//graph visualization
xtitle("generation of topology in Grid using BFS plot for 5
    lines and 5 columns.","X-Nodes","Y-Nodes");
i=NL_F_RandInt1n(length(TopologyGraph.node_x));//selection of
    the source node
display=10;//display parameter
WindowNumber=2;//window index
//2. generation of BFS plot.
[go,v,pred]=NL_R_BFSPlot(TopologyGraph,i,display,WindowNumber)
    ;//application of NL_R_BFSPlot
xtitle("generation of BFS plot for 5 lines and 5 columns.","X-
    Nodes","Y-Nodes");
i
v(1:10)//first ten values
pred(1:10)//first ten values
disp(go,v,pred);


//generation of graph using 6 lines and 9 columns
//1. generation of topology in Grid using BFS plot.
//2. generation of BFS plot.
lines=6;//number of lines
columns=9;//number of columns
links=5;// maximum of 5 links are created for any created node
x_area=1000;//network area x-side
y_area=1000;//network area x-side
//1.generation of topology in Grid using BFS plot.
display=10;//display parameter
WindowNumber=3;//window index
[TopologyGraph]=NL_T_Grid(lines,columns,x_area,y_area);//
    application of NL_T_Grid
```

```
VisualizeNodesEdges=NL_G_ShowGraphNE(TopologyGraph,WindowNumber
    );//graph visualization
xtitle("generation of topology in Grid using BFS plot for 6
    lines and 9 columns.","X-Nodes","Y-Nodes");
i=NL_F_RandInt1n(length(TopologyGraph.node_x));//selection of
    the source node
display=10;//display parameter
WindowNumber=4;//window index
//2. generation of BFS plot.
[go,v,pred]=NL_R_BFSPlot(TopologyGraph,i,display,WindowNumber)
    ;//application of NL_R_BFSPlot
xtitle("generation of BFS plot for 6 lines and 9 columns.","X-
    Nodes","Y-Nodes");
i
v(1:10)//first ten values
pred(1:10)//first ten values
disp(go,v,pred);


//generation of graph using 5 lines and 5 columns
//1. generation of topology in Grid using BFS plot.
//2. generation of BFS plot.
lines=10;//number of lines
columns=10;//number of columns
links=5;// maximum of 5 links are created for any created node
x_area=1000;//network area x-side
y_area=1000;//network area x-side
//1.generation of topology in Grid using BFS plot.
display=10;//display parameter
WindowNumber=5;//window index
[TopologyGraph]=NL_T_Grid(lines,columns,x_area,y_area);//
    application of NL_T_Grid
VisualizeNodesEdges=NL_G_ShowGraphNE(TopologyGraph,WindowNumber
    );//graph visualization
xtitle("generation of topology in Grid using BFS plot for 10
    lines and 10 columns.","X-Nodes","Y-Nodes");
i=NL_F_RandInt1n(length(TopologyGraph.node_x));//selection of
    the source node
display=10;//display parameter
WindowNumber=6;//window index
//2. generation of BFS plot.
[go,v,pred]=NL_R_BFSPlot(TopologyGraph,i,display,WindowNumber)
    ;//application of NL_R_BFSPlot
xtitle("generation of BFS plot for 10 lines and 10 columns.","X
    -Nodes","Y-Nodes");
i
v(1:10)//first ten values
pred(1:10)//first ten values
disp(go,v,pred);
```

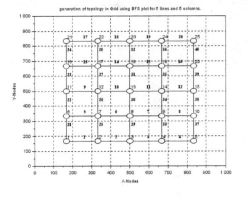

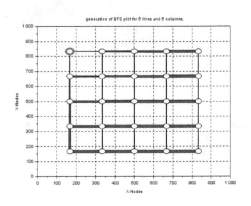

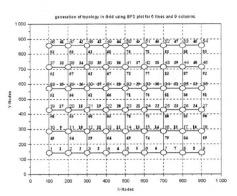

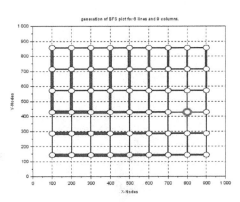

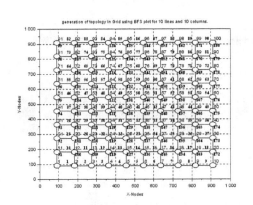

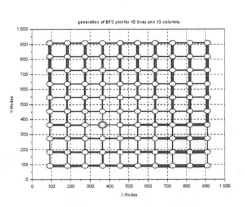

2.3 Generation of topology in barabasi alebert using BFS Plot

```
//This graph is to apply BFS to a random source node and
    display the corresponding graphs.
//generation of graph using number of nodes per layer as [5 10
    10 20]
//1. generation of topology in Multilevel using BFS plot.
//2. generation of BFS plot.

//1. generation of topology in Multilevel using BFS plot.
first_parameter=[0.3 0.3 0.3 0.3];//first parameter of the
    Waxman model for each network layer
second_parameter=[0.9 0.7 0.5 0.3];//second parameter of the
    Waxman model for each network layer
nodes_quantity=[5 10 10 20];//quantity of nodes per network
    layer
square_area=[1000 150 100 40];//squared area side per network
    layer
sub_nodes=[3 5 3 3];//maximal quantity of nodes per subnetwork
    for each layer
layer=4;//quantity of network layers
diameter_nodes=20;//original diameter of nodes
diameter_difference=5;//diameter difference between successive
    network layers
color=[2 5 6 1];//color of each network layer
i=NL_F_RandInt1n(length(TopologyGraph.node_x));//selection of
    the source node
display=5;//display parameter
WindowNumber=1;//window index
[TopologyGraph,d,nl]=NL_T_MultiLevel(first_parameter,
    second_parameter,nodes_quantity,square_area,sub_nodes,layer,
    diameter_nodes,diameter_difference,color);//application of
    NL_T_MultiLevel
VisualizeNodesEdges=NL_G_ShowGraph(TopologyGraph,WindowNumber)
    ;//graph visualization
xtitle("generation of topology in Multilevel using BFS plot for
    number of nodes per layer as [5 10 10 20]","X-Nodes","Y-
    Nodes");
//2. generation of BFS plot.

WindowNumber=2;//window index
[go,v,pred]=NL_R_BFSPlot(TopologyGraph,i,display,WindowNumber)
    ;//application of NL_R_BFSPlot
xtitle("generation of topology in barabasi alebert using BFS
    plot for number of nodes per layer as [5 10 10 20]","X-Nodes
    ","Y-Nodes");
i
```

```
v(1:10)//first ten values
pred(1:10)//first ten values
disp(go,v,pred);// to display the values in console


//generation of graph using number of nodes per layer as [20 30
    30 50]
//1. generation of topology in Multilevel using BFS plot.
//2. generation of BFS plot.

//1. generation of topology in Multilevel using BFS plot.
first_parameter=[0.3 0.3 0.3 0.3];//first parameter of the
    Waxman model for each network layer
second_parameter=[0.9 0.7 0.5 0.3];//second parameter of the
    Waxman model for each network layer
nodes_quantity=[20 30 30 50];//quantity of nodes per network
    layer
square_area=[1000 150 100 40];//squared area side per network
    layer
sub_nodes=[3 5 3 3];//maximal quantity of nodes per subnetwork
    for each layer
layer=4;//quantity of network layers
diameter_nodes=20;//original diameter of nodes
diameter_difference=5;//diameter difference between successive
    network layers
color=[2 5 6 1];//color of each network layer
i=NL_F_RandInt1n(length(TopologyGraph.node_x));//selection of
    the source node
display=5;//display parameter
WindowNumber=3;//window index
[TopologyGraph,d,nl]=NL_T_MultiLevel(first_parameter,
    second_parameter,nodes_quantity,square_area,sub_nodes,layer,
    diameter_nodes,diameter_difference,color);//application of
    NL_T_MultiLevel
VisualizeNodesEdges=NL_G_ShowGraph(TopologyGraph,WindowNumber)
    ;//graph visualization
xtitle("generation of topology in Multilevel using BFS plot for
    number of nodes per layer as [20 30 30 50]","X-Nodes","Y-
    Nodes");
//2. generation of BFS plot.

WindowNumber=4;//window index
[go,v,pred]=NL_R_BFSPlot(TopologyGraph,i,display,WindowNumber)
    ;//application of NL_R_BFSPlot
xtitle("generation of topology in barabasi alebert using BFS
    plot for number of nodes per layer as [20 30 30 50]","X-
    Nodes","Y-Nodes");
i
v(1:10)//first ten values
pred(1:10)//first ten values
```

```
disp(go,v,pred);// to display the values in console


//generation of graph using number of nodes per layer as [50
    100 100 150]
//1. generation of topology in Multilevel using BFS plot.
//2. generation of BFS plot.

//1. generation of topology in Multilevel using BFS plot.
first_parameter=[0.3 0.3 0.3 0.3];//first parameter of the
    Waxman model for each network layer
second_parameter=[0.9 0.7 0.5 0.3];//second parameter of the
    Waxman model for each network layer
nodes_quantity=[50 100 100 150];//quantity of nodes per network
     layer
square_area=[1000 150 100 40];//squared area side per network
    layer
sub_nodes=[3 5 3 3];//maximal quantity of nodes per subnetwork
    for each layer
layer=4;//quantity of network layers
diameter_nodes=20;//original diameter of nodes
diameter_difference=5;//diameter difference between successive
    network layers
color=[2 5 6 1];//color of each network layer
i=NL_F_RandInt1n(length(TopologyGraph.node_x));//selection of
    the source node
display=5;//display parameter
WindowNumber=5;//window index
[TopologyGraph,d,nl]=NL_T_MultiLevel(first_parameter,
    second_parameter,nodes_quantity,square_area,sub_nodes,layer,
    diameter_nodes,diameter_difference,color);//application of
    NL_T_MultiLevel
VisualizeNodesEdges=NL_G_ShowGraph(TopologyGraph,WindowNumber)
    ;//graph visualization
xtitle("generation of topology in Multilevel using BFS plot for
     number of nodes per layer as [50 100 100 150]","X-Nodes","Y
    -Nodes");
//2. generation of BFS plot.

WindowNumber=6;//window index
[go,v,pred]=NL_R_BFSPlot(TopologyGraph,i,display,WindowNumber)
    ;//application of NL_R_BFSPlot
xtitle("generation of topology in barabasi alebert using BFS
    plot for number of nodes per layer as [50 100 100 150]","X-
    Nodes","Y-Nodes");
i
v(1:10)//first ten values
pred(1:10)//first ten values
disp(go,v,pred);// to display the values in console
```

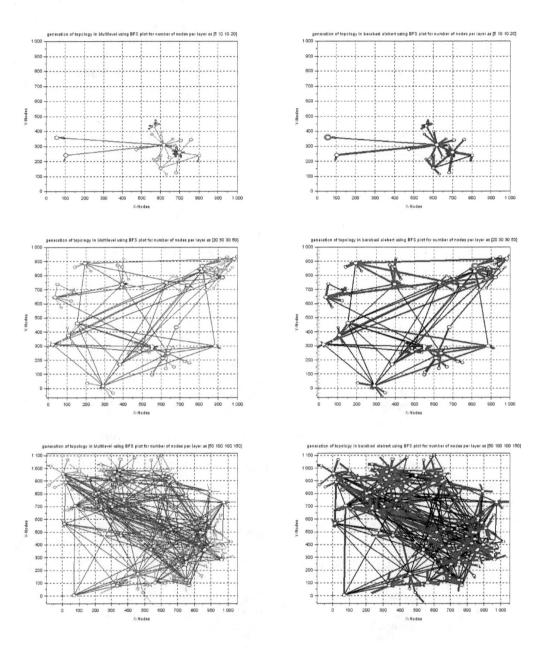

2.4   Generation of topology using waxmanconnex

```
//This graph is to apply BFS to a random source node and
    display the corresponding graphs.

//1.generation of topology using waxmanconnex
//2.generation of BFS weighted graph for waxmanconnex topology
//3.generation of topology using barbasialbert
//4.generation of BFS weighted graph for waxmanconnex topology

//generation of topologies and BFSweight for 25 nodes
firstparameter=0.1;//first parameter of the Waxman model
secondparameter=0.8;//second parameter of the Waxman model
NumberOfNodes=25;//number of nodes
area=1000;//network squared area side
links=5;//a maximum of 5 links are created for any created node
localityradius=100;//Locality radius

//1.generation of topology using waxmanconnex
display=5;//display parameter
WindowNumber=1;//window index
[TopologyGraph]=NL_T_WaxmanConnex(firstparameter,
    secondparameter,NumberOfNodes,area);//application of
    NL_T_WaxmanConnex
VisualizeNodesEdges=NL_G_ShowGraphE(TopologyGraph,WindowNumber)
    ;
xtitle("generation of topology using waxmanconnex for 25 nodes"
    );
i=NL_F_RandInt1n(length(TopologyGraph.node_x));//selection of
    the source node

//2.generation of BFS weighted graph for waxmanconnex topology
display=5;//display parameter
WindowNumber=2;//window index
[v,pred]=NL_R_BFSWeight(TopologyGraph,i);//application of
    NL_R_BFSWeight
i
v(1:10)//first ten values
pred(1:10)//first ten value
disp(v,pred);

//3.generation of topology using barbasialbert
[TopologyGraph,NodeDiameter]=NL_T_BarabasiAlbert(NumberOfNodes,
    links,area);//application of NL_T_BarabasiAlbert
WindowNumber=3;//window index
VisualizeNodesEdges=NL_G_ShowGraphE(TopologyGraph,WindowNumber)
    ;//graph visualization
xtitle("generation of topology using barbasialbert for 25 nodes
    ");
```

```
i=NL_F_RandInt1n(length(TopologyGraph.node_x));//selection of
    the source node
//4.generation of BFSweightplot graph for barbasialbert
    topology
display=5;//display parameter
WindowNumber=4;//window index
[v,pred]=NL_R_BFSWeight(TopologyGraph,i);//application of
    NL_R_BFSWeightPlot
i
v(1:10)//first ten values
pred(1:10)//first ten values




//generation of topologies and BFSweight for 50 nodes
firstparameter=0.1;//first parameter of the Waxman model
secondparameter=0.8;//second parameter of the Waxman model
NumberOfNodes=50;//number of nodes
area=1000;//network squared area side
links=5;//a maximum of 5 links are created for any created node
localityradius=100;//Locality radius

//1.generation of topology using waxmanconnex for 50 nodes
diaplay=5;//display parameter
WindowNumber=5;//window index
[TopologyGraph]=NL_T_WaxmanConnex(firstparameter,
    secondparameter,NumberOfNodes,area);//application of
    NL_T_WaxmanConnex
VisualizeNodesEdges=NL_G_ShowGraphE(TopologyGraph,WindowNumber)
    ;
xtitle("generation of topology using waxmanconnex for 50 nodes"
    );
i=NL_F_RandInt1n(length(TopologyGraph.node_x));//selection of
    the source node

//2.generation of BFS weighted graph for waxmanconnex topology
display=5;//display parameter
WindowNumber=6;//window index
[v,pred]=NL_R_BFSWeight(TopologyGraph,i);//application of
    NL_R_BFSWeight
i
v(1:10)//first ten values
pred(1:10)//first ten value
disp(v,pred);

//3.generation of topology using barbasialbert for 50 nodes
[TopologyGraph,NodeDiameter]=NL_T_BarabasiAlbert(NumberOfNodes,
    links,area);//application of NL_T_BarabasiAlbert
WindowNumber=7;//window index
```

```
VisualizeNodesEdges=NL_G_ShowGraphE(TopologyGraph,WindowNumber)
    ;//graph visualization
xtitle("generation of topology using barbasialbert for 50 nodes
    ");
i=NL_F_RandInt1n(length(TopologyGraph.node_x));//selection of
    the source node
//4.generation of BFSweightplot graph for barbasialbert
    topology
display=5;//display parameter
WindowNumber=8;//window index
[v,pred]=NL_R_BFSWeight(TopologyGraph,i);//application of
    NL_R_BFSWeightPlot
i
v(1:10)//first ten values
pred(1:10)//first ten values


//generation of topologies and bfsweight for 75 nodes
firstparameter=0.1;//first parameter of the Waxman model
secondparameter=0.8;//second parameter of the Waxman model
NumberOfNodes=75;//number of nodes
area=1000;//network squared area side
links=5;//a maximum of 5 links are created for any created node
localityradius=100;//Locality radius

//1.generation of topology using waxmanconnex for 75 nodes
display=5;//display parameter
WindowNumber=9;//window index
[TopologyGraph]=NL_T_WaxmanConnex(firstparameter,
    secondparameter,NumberOfNodes,area);//application of
    NL_T_WaxmanConnex
VisualizeNodesEdges=NL_G_ShowGraphE(TopologyGraph,WindowNumber)
    ;
xtitle("generation of topology using waxmanconnex for 75 nodes"
    );
i=NL_F_RandInt1n(length(TopologyGraph.node_x));//selection of
    the source node

//2.generation of BFS weighted graph for waxmanconnex topology
display=5;//display parameter
WindowNumber=10;//window index
[v,pred]=NL_R_BFSWeight(TopologyGraph,i);//application of
    NL_R_BFSWeight
i
v(1:10)//first ten values
pred(1:10)//first ten value
disp(v,pred);

//3.generation of topology using barbasialbert for 75 nodes
```

```
[TopologyGraph,NodeDiameter]=NL_T_BarabasiAlbert(NumberOfNodes,
    links,area);//application of NL_T_BarabasiAlbert
WindowNumber=11;//window index
VisualizeNodesEdges=NL_G_ShowGraphE(TopologyGraph,WindowNumber)
    ;//graph visualization
xtitle("generation of topology using barbasialbert for 75 nodes
    ");
i=NL_F_RandInt1n(length(TopologyGraph.node_x));//selection of
    the source node
//4.generation of BFSweightplot graph for barbasialbert
    topology
display=5;//display parameter
WindowNumber=12;//window index
[v,pred]=NL_R_BFSWeight(TopologyGraph,i);//application of
    NL_R_BFSWeightPlot
i
v(1:10)//first ten values
pred(1:10)//first ten values
```

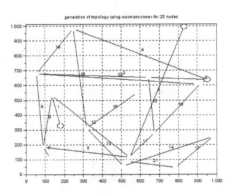

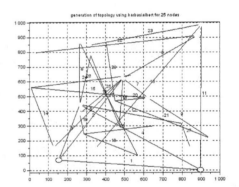

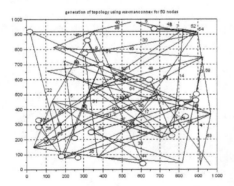

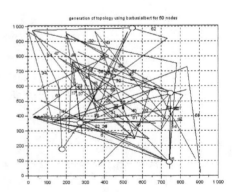

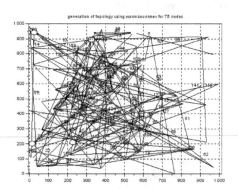

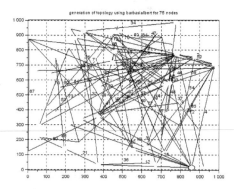

2.5 Generation of BFS weightplot graph for waxman-connex topology

```
//1.generation of topology using waxmanconnex
//2.generation of bfsweightplot graph for waxmanconnex topology
//3.generation of topology using barbasialbert
//4.generation of bfsweightplot graph for barbasialbert
    topology

//generation of topologies and bfsweightplot for 25 nodes
a=0.1;//first parameter of the Waxman model
b=0.8;//second parameter of the Waxman model
n=25;//number of nodes
l0=5;//a maximum of 5 links are created for any created node
l=1000;//network squared area side
dmax=100;//Locality radius

//1.generation of topology using waxmanconnex
dw=5;//display parameter
ind=1;//window index
[g]=NL_T_WaxmanConnex(a,b,n,l);//application of
    NL_T_WaxmanConnex
f=NL_G_ShowGraphE(g,ind);

i=NL_F_RandInt1n(length(g.node_x));//selection of the source
    node

//2.generation of bfsweightplot graph for waxmanconnex topology
dw=5;//display parameter
ind=3;//window index
[go,v,pred]=NL_R_BFSWeightPlot(g,i,dw,ind);//application of
    NL_R_BFSWeightPlot
i
v(1:10)//first ten values
pred(1:10)//first ten values

//3.generation of topology using barbasialbert
[g,d]=NL_T_BarabasiAlbert(n,l0,l);//application of
    NL_T_BarabasiAlbert
ind=4;//window index
f=NL_G_ShowGraphN(g,ind);//graph visualization

//4.generation of bfsweightplot graph for barbasialbert
    topology
dw=5;//display parameter
ind=5;//window index
[go,v,pred]=NL_R_BFSWeightPlot(g,i,dw,ind);//application of
    NL_R_BFSWeightPlot
```

```
i
v(1:10)//first ten values
pred(1:10)//first ten values


//generation of topologies and bfsweightplot for 50 nodes
a=0.1;//first parameter of the Waxman model
b=0.8;//second parameter of the Waxman model
n=50;//number of nodes
lo=5;//a maximum of 5 links are created for any created node
l=1000;//network squared area side
dmax=100;//Locality radius

//1.generation of topology using waxmanconnex
dw=5;//display parameter
ind=6;//window index
[g]=NL_T_WaxmanConnex(a,b,n,l);//application of
    NL_T_WaxmanConnex
f=NL_G_ShowGraphE(g,ind);

i=NL_F_RandInt1n(length(g.node_x));//selection of the source
    node

//2.generation of bfsweightplot graph for waxmanconnex topology
dw=5;//display parameter
ind=8;//window index
[go,v,pred]=NL_R_BFSWeightPlot(g,i,dw,ind);//application of
    NL_R_BFSWeightPlot
i
v(1:10)//first ten values
pred(1:10)//first ten values

//3.generation of topology using barbasialbert
[g,d]=NL_T_BarabasiAlbert(n,lo,l);//application of
    NL_T_BarabasiAlbert
ind=9;//window index
f=NL_G_ShowGraphN(g,ind);//graph visualization

//4.generation of bfsweightplot graph for barbasialbert
    topology
dw=5;//display parameter
ind=10;//window index
[go,v,pred]=NL_R_BFSWeightPlot(g,i,dw,ind);//application of
    NL_R_BFSWeightPlot
i
v(1:10)//first ten values
pred(1:10)//first ten values


//generation of topologies and bfsweightplot for 75 nodes
```

```
a=0.1;//first parameter of the Waxman model
b=0.8;//second parameter of the Waxman model
n=75;//number of nodes
l0=5;//a maximum of 5 links are created for any created node
l=1000;//network squared area side
dmax=100;//Locality radius

//1.generation of topology using waxmanconnex
dw=5;//display parameter
ind=11;//window index
[g]=NL_T_WaxmanConnex(a,b,n,l);//application of
    NL_T_WaxmanConnex
f=NL_G_ShowGraphE(g,ind);

i=NL_F_RandInt1n(length(g.node_x));//selection of the source
    node

//2.generation of bfsweightplot graph for waxmanconnex topology
dw=5;//display parameter
ind=13;//window index
[go,v,pred]=NL_R_BFSWeightPlot(g,i,dw,ind);//application of
    NL_R_BFSWeightPlot
i
v(1:10)//first ten values
pred(1:10)//first ten values

//3.generation of topology using barbasialbert
[g,d]=NL_T_BarabasiAlbert(n,l0,l);//application of
    NL_T_BarabasiAlbert
ind=14;//window index
f=NL_G_ShowGraphN(g,ind);//graph visualization

//4.generation of bfsweightplot graph for barbasialbert
    topology
dw=5;//display parameter
ind=15;//window index
[go,v,pred]=NL_R_BFSWeightPlot(g,i,dw,ind);//application of
    NL_R_BFSWeightPlot
i
v(1:10)//first ten values
pred(1:10)//first ten values
```

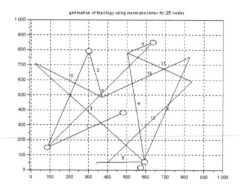

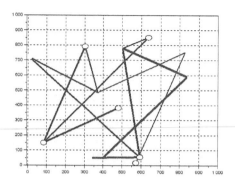

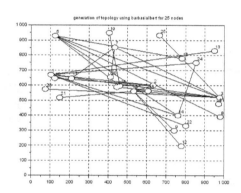

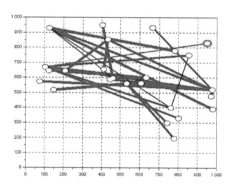

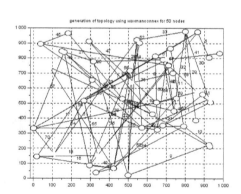

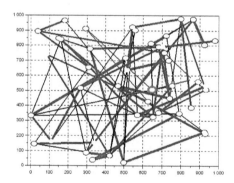

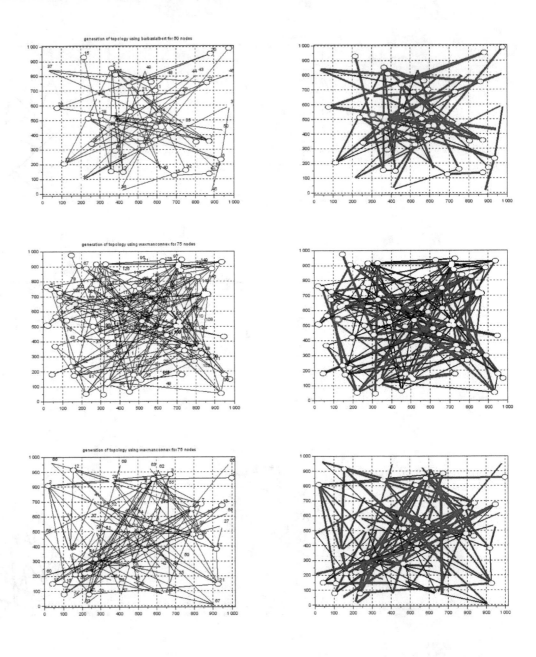

2.6   Generation of locality connex

```
//Ths graph is to update the vector of candidates where to
    propagate the topology discovery tree from a current node in
    respect with the node index (BFS-Start)
//1.Generation of locality connex
//2.Displaying edge data fields
//3.Generation of BFSSearchStart for grid topology
//4.Connecting a Waxman subnetwork around a node of the graph


//FIRST GRAPH
//1.generation of locality connex
NumberOfNodes=70;//number of nodes
NetworkSquaredAreaSide=1000;//network squared area side
LocalityRadius=100;//Locality radius
[Graph]=NL_T_LocalityConnex(NumberOfNodes,
    NetworkSquaredAreaSide,LocalityRadius);//generation of a
    topology
WindowNumber=1;//window index
[f]=NL_G_ShowGraphE(Graph,WindowNumber);//graph visualization
xtitle("Locality Connex","X-Nodes","Y-Nodes");
//2.displaying edge data fields
[edge_head,edge_tail,edge_color,edge_width,edge_length,
    edge_weight,edge_number]=NL_G_EdgeDataFields(Graph)//
    application of NL_G_EdgeDataFields

//3.generation of BFSSearchStart for grid topology
NumberOfGridLines =10;//number of grid lines
NumberOfGridColumns=7;//number of grid columns
NetworkAreaX=1000;//network area x-side
NetworkAreaY=1000;//network area y-side
[g]=NL_T_Grid(NumberOfGridLines,NumberOfGridColumns,
    NetworkAreaX,NetworkAreaY);//application of NL_T_Grid
NL_G_ShowGraphNE(g,2);//graph visualization
xtitle("Grid Topology","X-Nodes","Y-Nodes");
//4.Connecting a Waxman subnetwork around a node of the graph
nr=length(g.node_x);//real network size
nl=length(g.head);
i=NL_F_RandInt1n(length(g.node_x));//selection of the source
    node

a=0.1;//waxman parameters
b=0.1;
QunatityOfNodes=20;//quantity of nodes of the new subnetwork
Radius=150;//maximal radius between new nodes and the central
    node
[ge]=NL_T_AddWaxman2Node(a,b,QunatityOfNodes,Radius,g,i);//
    application of NL_T_AddWaxman2Node
```

```
gl=length(g.head);//visualization parameters
gel=length(ge.head);
gn=length(g.node_x);//real network size
gen=length(ge.node_x);
ec=5*ones(1,gel);
ec(1:gl)=ones(1,gl);//edge color
nc=5*ones(1,gen);
nc(1:gn)=ones(1,gn);//node color
ge.edge_color=ec;
ge.node_color=nc;
WindowIndex=3;//window index
f=NL_G_ShowGraph(ge,WindowIndex);//graph visualization
xtitle("Waxman Node","X-Nodes","Y-Nodes");
pred=zeros(1,n);//initialization
visited=[];//visited
candidates=[];//candidates
[visited,candidates,pred]=NL_R_BFSSearchStart(i,g,visited,
    candidates,pred);//application of NL_R_BFSSearchStart
p=[];//display the candidates, the first ones are represented
    with the smallest edge width
for i=1:length(candidates)
p=[p NL_G_Nodes2Path([visited candidates(i)],g)];
end
Bdi=5;
Ebi=2;
EC=ones(1,nl);//edge color
EB=Ebi*ones(2,nl);//edge width
EC(p)=5;
EB(p)=Ebi*(1:length(p));
D=Bdi*ones(1,nr);//node border
D([visited candidates])=2*Bdi;//node border calculation
g.node_border=D;//assigning node border
g.edge_color=EC;//assigning edge color
g.edge_width=EB;//assigning edge width
WindowIndex=4;//window index
[f]=NL_G_ShowGraphN(g,WindowIndex);//graph visualization
xtitle("Edge Coloring","X-Nodes","Y-Nodes");
//SECOND GRAPH


//1.generation of locality connex
NumberOfNodes=150;//number of nodes
NetworkSquaredAreaSide=1000;//network squared area side
LocalityRadius=100;//Locality radius
[Graph]=NL_T_LocalityConnex(NumberOfNodes,
    NetworkSquaredAreaSide,LocalityRadius);//generation of a
    topology
WindowNumber=5;//window index
[f]=NL_G_ShowGraphE(Graph,WindowNumber);//graph visualization
xtitle("Locality Connex","X-Nodes","Y-Nodes");
```

```
//2.displaying edge data fields
[edge_head,edge_tail,edge_color,edge_width,edge_length,
    edge_weight,edge_number]=NL_G_EdgeDataFields(Graph)//
    application of NL_G_EdgeDataFields

//3.generation of BFSSearchStart for grid topology
NumberOfGridLines =10;//number of grid lines
NumberOfGridColumns=7;//number of grid columns
NetworkAreaX=1000;//network area x-side
NetworkAreaY=1000;//network area y-side
[g]=NL_T_Grid(NumberOfGridLines,NumberOfGridColumns,
    NetworkAreaX,NetworkAreaY);//application of NL_T_Grid
NL_G_ShowGraphNE(g,6);//graph visualization
xtitle("Grid Topology","X-Nodes","Y-Nodes");
//4.Connecting a Waxman subnetwork around a node of the graph
nr=length(g.node_x);//real network size
nl=length(g.head);
i=NL_F_RandInt1n(length(g.node_x));//selection of the source
    node

a=0.1;//waxman parameters
b=0.1;
QunatityOfNodes=20;//quantity of nodes of the new subnetwork
Radius=150;//maximal radius between new nodes and the central
    node
[ge]=NL_T_AddWaxman2Node(a,b,QunatityOfNodes,Radius,g,i);//
    application of NL_T_AddWaxman2Node
gl=length(g.head);//visualization parameters
gel=length(ge.head);
gn=length(g.node_x);//real network size
gen=length(ge.node_x);
ec=5*ones(1,gel);
ec(1:gl)=ones(1,gl);//edge color
nc=5*ones(1,gen);
nc(1:gn)=ones(1,gn);//node color
ge.edge_color=ec;
ge.node_color=nc;
WindowIndex=7;//window index
f=NL_G_ShowGraph(ge,WindowIndex);//graph visualization
xtitle("Waxman Node","X-Nodes","Y-Nodes");
pred=zeros(1,n);//initialization
visited=[];//visited
candidates=[];//candidates
[visited,candidates,pred]=NL_R_BFSSearchStart(i,g,visited,
    candidates,pred);//application of NL_R_BFSSearchStart
p=[];//display the candidates, the first ones are represented
    with the smallest edge width
for i=1:length(candidates)
p=[p NL_G_Nodes2Path([visited candidates(i)],g)];
end
```

```
Bdi=5;
Ebi=2;
EC=ones(1,nl);//edge color
EB=Ebi*ones(2,nl);//edge width
EC(p)=5;
EB(p)=Ebi*(1:length(p));
D=Bdi*ones(1,nr);//node border
D([visited candidates])=2*Bdi;//node border calculation
g.node_border=D;//assigning node border
g.edge_color=EC;//assigning edge color
g.edge_width=EB;//assigning edge width
WindowIndex=8;//window index
[f]=NL_G_ShowGraphN(g,WindowIndex);//graph visualization
xtitle("Edge Coloring","X-Nodes","Y-Nodes");
```

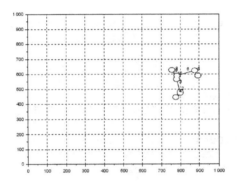
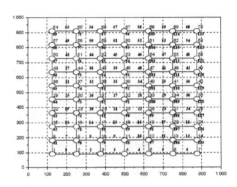

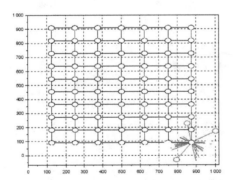
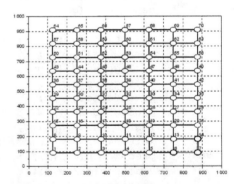

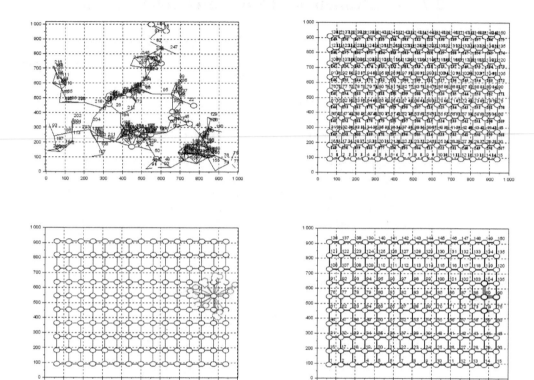

2.7   Generation of BFSWSearchStart for grid topology

```
//This program is to update the vector of candidates where to
    propagate the topology discovery tree from a current node in
    respect with the node index (Start).
//1.Generation of Locality Connex
//2.Displaying edge data fields
//3.Generation of BFSWSearchStart for grid topology
//4.Connecting a Waxman subnetwork around a node of the graph

//FIRST GRAPH
//1.generation of locality connex
NumberOfNodes=70;//number of nodes
NetworkSquaredAreaSide=1000;//network squared area side
LocalityRadius=100;//Locality radius
[Graph]=NL_T_LocalityConnex(NumberOfNodes,
    NetworkSquaredAreaSide,LocalityRadius);//generation of a
    topology
WindowNumber=1;//window index
[f]=NL_G_ShowGraphE(Graph,WindowNumber);//graph visualization
xtitle("Locality Connex","X-Nodes","Y-Nodes");
//2.displaying edge data fields
[edge_head,edge_tail,edge_color,edge_width,edge_length,
    edge_weight,edge_number]=NL_G_EdgeDataFields(Graph)//
    application of NL_G_EdgeDataFields

//3.generation of BFSSearchStart for grid topology
NumberOfGridLines =10;//number of grid lines
NumberOfGridColumns=7;//number of grid columns
NetworkAreaX=1000;//network area x-side
NetworkAreaY=1000;//network area y-side
[g]=NL_T_Grid(NumberOfGridLines,NumberOfGridColumns,
    NetworkAreaX,NetworkAreaY);//application of NL_T_Grid
NL_G_ShowGraphNE(g,2);//graph visualization
xtitle("Grid Topology","X-Nodes","Y-Nodes");
//4.Connecting a Waxman subnetwork around a node of the graph
nr=length(g.node_x);//real network size
nl=length(g.head);
i=NL_F_RandInt1n(length(g.node_x));//selection of the source
    node

//4.Connecting a Waxman subnetwork around a node of the graph
a=0.1;//waxman parameters
b=0.1;
QunatityOfNodes=20;//quantity of nodes of the new subnetwork
Radius=150;//maximal radius between new nodes and the central
    node
[ge]=NL_T_AddWaxman2Node(a,b,QunatityOfNodes,Radius,g,i);//
    application of NL_T_AddWaxman2Node
```

```
gl=length(g.head);//visualization parameters
gel=length(ge.head);
gn=length(g.node_x);//real network size
gen=length(ge.node_x);
ec=5*ones(1,gel);
ec(1:gl)=ones(1,gl);//edge color
nc=5*ones(1,gen);
nc(1:gn)=ones(1,gn);//node color
ge.edge_color=ec;
ge.node_color=nc;
WindowIndex=3;//window index
f=NL_G_ShowGraph(ge,WindowIndex);//graph visualization

nr=length(g.node_x);//real network size
nl=length(g.head);
i=NL_F_RandInt1n(length(g.node_x));//selection of the source
    node
pred=zeros(1,n);//initialization
visited=[];//visited
candidates=[];//candidates
[d,dv]=NL_G_GraphDegreeDist(g);//calculation of the node degree
    distribution
[visited,candidates,pred]=NL_R_BFSWSearchStart(i,g,dv,visited,
    candidates,pred);//application of NL_R_BFSWeightSearchStart
p=[];//display the candidates, the first ones are represented
    with the smallest edge width
for i=1:length(candidates)
p=[p NL_G_Nodes2Path([visited candidates(i)],g)];
end
Bdi=5;
Ebi=2;
EC=ones(1,nl);//edge color
EB=Ebi*ones(1,nl);//edge width
EC(p)=5;
EB(p)=Ebi*(1:length(p));
D=Bdi*ones(1,nr);//node border
D([v candidates])=2*Bdi;
g.node_border=D;
g.edge_color=EC;
g.edge_width=EB;
WindowIndex=4;//window index
[f]=NL_G_ShowGraphN(g,WindowIndex);//graph visualization
i
visited
candidates
pred

//SECOND GRAPH

//1.generation of locality connex
```

```
NumberOfNodes=150;//number of nodes
NetworkSquaredAreaSide=1000;//network squared area side
LocalityRadius=100;//Locality radius
[Graph]=NL_T_LocalityConnex(NumberOfNodes,
    NetworkSquaredAreaSide,LocalityRadius);//generation of a
    topology
WindowNumber=5;//window index
[f]=NL_G_ShowGraphE(Graph,WindowNumber);//graph visualization
xtitle("Locality Connex","X-Nodes","Y-Nodes");
//2.displaying edge data fields
[edge_head,edge_tail,edge_color,edge_width,edge_length,
    edge_weight,edge_number]=NL_G_EdgeDataFields(Graph)//
    application of NL_G_EdgeDataFields

//3.generation of BFSSearchStart for grid topology
NumberOfGridLines =10;//number of grid lines
NumberOfGridColumns=7;//number of grid columns
NetworkAreaX=1000;//network area x-side
NetworkAreaY=1000;//network area y-side
[g]=NL_T_Grid(NumberOfGridLines,NumberOfGridColumns,
    NetworkAreaX,NetworkAreaY);//application of NL_T_Grid
NL_G_ShowGraphNE(g,6);//graph visualization
xtitle("Grid Topology","X-Nodes","Y-Nodes");
//4.Connecting a Waxman subnetwork around a node of the graph
nr=length(g.node_x);//real network size
nl=length(g.head);
i=NL_F_RandInt1n(length(g.node_x));//selection of the source
    node

//4.Connecting a Waxman subnetwork around a node of the graph
a=0.1;//waxman parameters
b=0.1;
QunatityOfNodes=20;//quantity of nodes of the new subnetwork
Radius=150;//maximal radius between new nodes and the central
    node
[ge]=NL_T_AddWaxman2Node(a,b,QunatityOfNodes,Radius,g,i);//
    application of NL_T_AddWaxman2Node
gl=length(g.head);//visualization parameters
gel=length(ge.head);
gn=length(g.node_x);//real network size
gen=length(ge.node_x);
ec=5*ones(1,gel);
ec(1:gl)=ones(1,gl);//edge color
nc=5*ones(1,gen);
nc(1:gn)=ones(1,gn);//node color
ge.edge_color=ec;
ge.node_color=nc;
WindowIndex=7;//window index
f=NL_G_ShowGraph(ge,WindowIndex);//graph visualization
```

```
nr=length(g.node_x);//real network size
nl=length(g.head);
i=NL_F_RandInt1n(length(g.node_x));//selection of the source
    node
pred=zeros(1,n);//initialization
visited=[];//visited
candidates=[];//candidates
[d,dv]=NL_G_GraphDegreeDist(g);//calculation of the node degree
    distribution
[visited,candidates,pred]=NL_R_BFSWSearchStart(i,g,dv,visited,
    candidates,pred);//application of NL_R_BFSWeightSearchStart
p=[];//display the candidates, the first ones are represented
    with the smallest edge width
for i=1:length(candidates)
p=[p NL_G_Nodes2Path([visited candidates(i)],g)];
end
Bdi=5;
Ebi=2;
EC=ones(1,nl);//edge color
EB=Ebi*ones(1,nl);//edge width
EC(p)=5;
EB(p)=Ebi*(1:length(p));
D=Bdi*ones(1,nr);//node border
D([v candidates])=2*Bdi;
g.node_border=D;
g.edge_color=EC;
g.edge_width=EB;
WindowIndex=8;//window index
[f]=NL_G_ShowGraphN(g,WindowIndex);//graph visualization
i
visited
candidates
pred
```

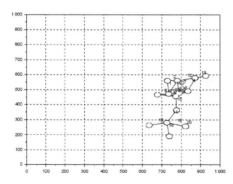
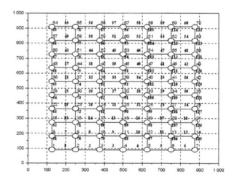

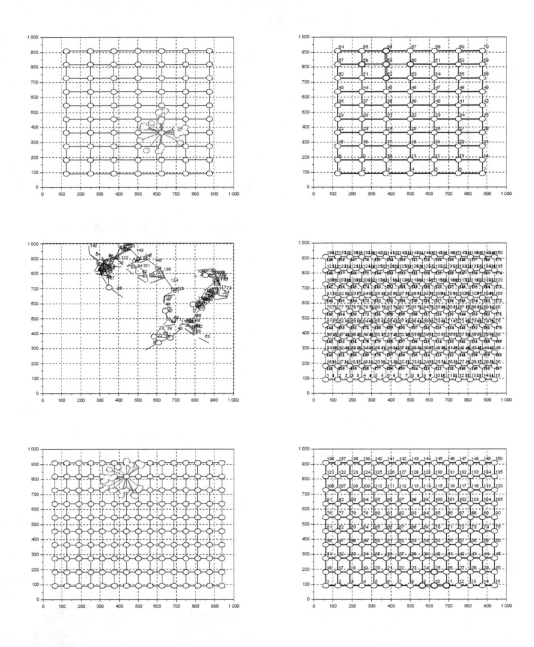

2.8   Generation of topology in barabasi alebert using DFS plot

```
//This graph is to apply DFS to a random source node and
    display the corresponding graphs.
//generation of plot using 10 nodes
//1.generation of topology in barabasi alebert using DFS plot
//2.generation of DFS plot.


NumberOfNodes=10;//number of nodes
links=3;//a maximum of 3 links are created for any created node
area=1000;//network square area side
localityradius=100;//Locality radius
display=5;
WindowNumber=1;//window index
//1. generation of topology in barabasi alebert using DFS plot
[TopologyGraph,NodeDiameter]=NL_T_BarabasiAlbert(NumberOfNodes,
    links,area);//application of NL_T_BarabasiAlbert

VisualizeNodesEdges=NL_G_ShowGraphN(TopologyGraph,WindowNumber)
    ;//graph visualization
xtitle("generation of topology in barabasi alebert using DFS
    plot for 10 nodes","X-Nodes","Y-Nodes");
i=NL_F_RandInt1n(length(TopologyGraph.node_x));//selection of
    the source node

display=5;//display parameter
WindowNumber=3;//window index

//2.generation of DFS plot
[go,v,pred]=NL_R_DFSPlot(TopologyGraph,i,display,WindowNumber)
    ;//application of NL_R_DFSPlot
xtitle("generation of DFS plot for 10 nodes","X-Nodes","Y-Nodes
    ");
i
v(1:10)//first ten values
pred(1:10)//first ten values
disp(go,v,pred);// to display the values in console


//generation of plot using 30 nodes
//1.generation of topology in barabasi alebert using DFS plot
//2.generation of DFS plot.

NumberOfNodes=30;//number of nodes
links=3;//a maximum of 3 links are created for any created node
area=1000;//network square area side
localityradius=100;//Locality radius
```

```
display=5;
WindowNumber=4;//window index
//1. generation of topology in barabasi alebert using DFS plot
[TopologyGraph,NodeDiameter]=NL_T_BarabasiAlbert(NumberOfNodes,
    links,area);//application of NL_T_BarabasiAlbert

VisualizeNodesEdges=NL_G_ShowGraphN(TopologyGraph,WindowNumber)
    ;//graph visualization
xtitle("generation topology in barabasi alebert using DFS plot
    for 30 nodes","X-Nodes","Y-Nodes");
i=NL_F_RandInt1n(length(TopologyGraph.node_x));//selection of
    the source node

display=5;//display parameter
WindowNumber=5;//window index

//3.generation of DFS plot
[go,v,pred]=NL_R_DFSPlot(TopologyGraph,i,display,WindowNumber)
    ;//application of NL_R_DFSPlot
xtitle("generation of DFS plot for 30 nodes","X-Nodes","Y-Nodes
    ");
i
v(1:10)//first ten values
pred(1:10)//first ten values
disp(go,v,pred);// to display the values in console

//generation of plot using 80 nodes
//1.generation of topology in barabasi alebert using DFS plot
//2.generation of DFS plot.

NumberOfNodes=80;//number of nodes
links=3;//a maximum of 3 links are created for any created node
area=1000;//network square area side
localityradius=100;//Locality radius
display=5;
WindowNumber=6;//window index
//1. generation of topology in barabasi alebert using DFS plot
[TopologyGraph,NodeDiameter]=NL_T_BarabasiAlbert(NumberOfNodes,
    links,area);//application of NL_T_BarabasiAlbert

VisualizeNodesEdges=NL_G_ShowGraphN(TopologyGraph,WindowNumber)
    ;//graph visualization
xtitle("generation topology in barabasi alebert using DFS plot
    for 80 nodes","X-Nodes","Y-Nodes");
i=NL_F_RandInt1n(length(TopologyGraph.node_x));//selection of
    the source node

display=5;//display parameter
WindowNumber=7;//window index
```

```
//3.generation of DFS plot
[go,v,pred]=NL_R_DFSPlot(TopologyGraph,i,display,WindowNumber)
    ;//application of NL_R_DFSPlot
xtitle("generation of DFS plot for 80 nodes","X-Nodes","Y-Nodes
    ");
i
v(1:10)//first ten values
pred(1:10)//first ten values
disp(go,v,pred);// to display the values in console
```

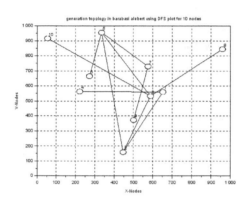

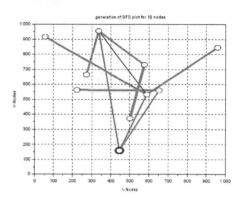

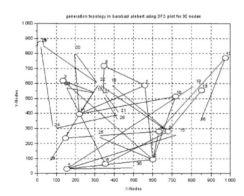

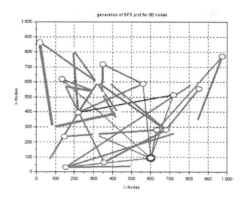

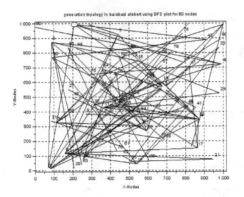

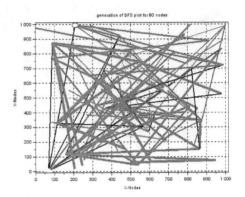

2.9   Generation of topology in MultiLevel using DFS plot

```
//This graph is to apply DFS to a random source node and
    display the corresponding graphs.
//generation of plot using 10 nodes
//1.generation of topology in MultiLevel using DFS plot
//2.generation of DFS plot
```

```
NumberOfNodes=10;//number of nodes
links=1000;//network square area side
NodeDiameter=100;//Locality radius
first_parameter=[0.3 0.3 0.3 0.3];//first parameter of the
    Waxman model for each network layer
second_parameter=[0.9 0.7 0.5 0.3];//second parameter of the
    Waxman model for each network layer
networklayer=[30 50 50 100];//quantity of nodes per network
    layer
areaside=[1000 150 100 40];//squared area side per network
    layer
NumberOfNodes=[3 5 3 3];//maximal quantity of nodes per
    subnetwork for each layer
quantity=4;//quantity of network layers
originaldiameter=20;//original diameter of nodes
diameterdifference=5;//diameter difference between successive
    network layers
colorofnetwork=[2 5 6 1];//color of each network layer

//1. generation of topology in multilevel using DFS plot
[TopologyGraph,d,networklayer]=NL_T_MultiLevel(first_parameter,
    second_parameter,networklayer,areaside,NumberOfNodes,
    quantity,originaldiameter,diameterdifference,colorofnetwork)
    ;//application of NL_T_MultiLevel

WindowNumber=2;//window index
VisualizeNodesEdges=NL_G_ShowGraph(TopologyGraph,WindowNumber)
    ;//graph visualization
xtitle("generation of topology in Multilevel using DFS plot for
    10 nodes","X-Nodes","Y-Nodes");
i=NL_F_RandInt1n(length(TopologyGraph.node_x));//selection of
    the source node
display=2;//display parameter
WindowNumber=3;//window index
//2.generation of DFS plot
[go,v,pred]=NL_R_DFSPlot(TopologyGraph,i,display,WindowNumber)
    ;//application of NL_R_DFSPlot
xtitle("generation of DFS plot for 10 nodes","X-Nodes","Y-Nodes
    ");
i
```

```
v(1:10)//first ten values
pred(1:10)//first ten values


//generation of plot using 50 nodes
//1.generation of topology in MultiLevel using DFS plot
//2.generation of DFS plot

NumberOfNodes=50;//number of nodes
links=1000;//network square area side
NodeDiameter=100;//Locality radius
first_parameter=[0.3 0.3 0.3 0.3];//first parameter of the
    Waxman model for each network layer
second_parameter=[0.9 0.7 0.5 0.3];//second parameter of the
    Waxman model for each network layer
networklayer=[30 50 50 100];//quantity of nodes per network
    layer
areaside=[1000 150 100 40];//squared area side per network
    layer
NumberOfNodes=[3 5 3 3];//maximal quantity of nodes per
    subnetwork for each layer
quantity=4;//quantity of network layers
originaldiameter=20;//original diameter of nodes
diameterdifference=5;//diameter difference between successive
    network layers
colorofnetwork=[2 5 6 1];//color of each network layer

//1. generation of topology in multilevel using DFS plot
[TopologyGraph,d,networklayer]=NL_T_MultiLevel(first_parameter,
    second_parameter,networklayer,areaside,NumberOfNodes,
    quantity,originaldiameter,diameterdifference,colorofnetwork)
    ;//application of NL_T_MultiLevel

WindowNumber=4;//window index
VisualizeNodesEdges=NL_G_ShowGraph(TopologyGraph,WindowNumber)
    ;//graph visualization
xtitle("generation of topology in Multilevel using DFS plot for
    50 nodes","X-Nodes","Y-Nodes");
i=NL_F_RandInt1n(length(TopologyGraph.node_x));//selection of
    the source node
display=2;//display parameter
WindowNumber=5;//window index
//2.generation of DFS plot
[go,v,pred]=NL_R_DFSPlot(TopologyGraph,i,display,WindowNumber)
    ;//application of NL_R_DFSPlot
xtitle("generation of DFS plot for 50 nodes","X-Nodes","Y-Nodes
    ");
i
v(1:10)//first ten values
pred(1:10)//first ten values
```

```
//generation of plot using 150 nodes
//1.generation of topology in MultiLevel using DFS plot
//2.generation of DFS plot


NumberOfNodes=150;//number of nodes
links=1000;//network square area side
NodeDiameter=100;//Locality radius
first_parameter=[0.3 0.3 0.3 0.3];//first parameter of the
    Waxman model for each network layer
second_parameter=[0.9 0.7 0.5 0.3];//second parameter of the
    Waxman model for each network layer
networklayer=[30 50 50 100];//quantity of nodes per network
    layer
areaside=[1000 150 100 40];//squared area side per network
    layer
NumberOfNodes=[3 5 3 3];//maximal quantity of nodes per
    subnetwork for each layer
quantity=4;//quantity of network layers
originaldiameter=20;//original diameter of nodes
diameterdifference=5;//diameter difference between successive
    network layers
colorofnetwork=[2 5 6 1];//color of each network layer

//1. generation of topology in multilevel using DFS plot
[TopologyGraph,d,networklayer]=NL_T_MultiLevel(first_parameter,
    second_parameter,networklayer,areaside,NumberOfNodes,
    quantity,originaldiameter,diameterdifference,colorofnetwork)
    ;//application of NL_T_MultiLevel

WindowNumber=6;//window index
VisualizeNodesEdges=NL_G_ShowGraph(TopologyGraph,WindowNumber)
    ;//graph visualization
xtitle("generation of topology in Multilevel using DFS plot for
    150 nodes","X-Nodes","Y-Nodes");
i=NL_F_RandInt1n(length(TopologyGraph.node_x));//selection of
    the source node
display=2;//display parameter
WindowNumber=7;//window index
//2.generation of DFS plot
[go,v,pred]=NL_R_DFSPlot(TopologyGraph,i,display,WindowNumber)
    ;//application of NL_R_DFSPlot
xtitle("generation of DFS plot for 150 nodes","X-Nodes","Y-
    Nodes");
i
v(1:10)//first ten values
pred(1:10)//first ten values
```

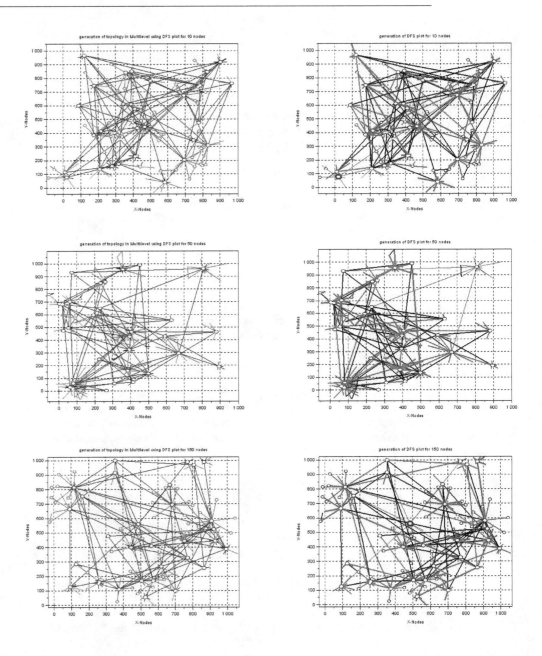

2.10   Generation of DFS search end for Waxman mode topology

```
//This graph is to apply DFS to a random source node and
    display the correspondung graphs
//1.Generation of topology using Waxman mode
//2.Generation of dfs_search_end for Waxman mode topology

NumberOfNodes=20;//number of nodes
area=1000;//network squared area side
localityradius=100;//Locality radius
first_parameter=0.1;//first parameter of the Waxman model
second_parameter=0.8;//second parameter of the Waxman model
//1.generation of topology using Waxman mode
display=5;//display parameter
WindowNumber=1;//window index
[TopologyGraph,localityradius]=NL_T_Waxman(first_parameter,
    second_parameter,NumberOfNodes,area);//application of
    NL_T_Waxman
VisualizeNodeEdges=NL_G_ShowGraphN(TopologyGraph,WindowNumber)
    ;//graph visualization
xtitle("generation of topology using Waxman mode");
WindowNumber=2;//window index
scf(WindowNumber);
clf(WindowNumber);
plot(localityradius);
plot2d3(localityradius);//graph visualization
nr=length(TopologyGraph.node_x);//real network size
nl=length(TopologyGraph.head);
i=NL_F_RandInt1n(length(TopologyGraph.node_x));//selection of
    the source node
pred=zeros(1,NumberOfNodes);//initialization
v=[];//visited
c=[];//candidates
[v,c,pred]=NL_R_DFSSearchEnd(i,TopologyGraph,v,c,pred);//
    application of NL_R_DFSSearchEnd
display_candidates=[];//display the candidates, the first ones
    are represented with the smallest edge width
for j=1:length(c)
display_candidates=[display_candidates NL_G_Nodes2Path([v c(j)
    ],TopologyGraph)];
end
Bdi=5;
Ebi=2;
EdgeColor=ones(1,nl);//edge color
EdgeWidth=Ebi*ones(1,nl);//edge width
EdgeColor(display_candidates)=5;
```

```
EdgeWidth(display_candidates)=Ebi*(1:length(display_candidates)
    );
node_border=Bdi*ones(1,nr);//node border
node_border([v c])=2*Bdi;
TopologyGraph.node_border=node_border;
TopologyGraph.edge_color=EdgeColor;
TopologyGraph.edge_width=EdgeWidth;
WindowNumber=3;//window index
[VisualizeNodeEdges]=NL_G_ShowGraphN(TopologyGraph,WindowNumber
    );//graph visualization
xtitle("Generation of dfs_search_end for Waxman mode topology")
    ;
i
v
c
pred


NumberOfNodes=50;//number of nodes
area=1000;//network squared area side
localityradius=100;//Locality radius
first_parameter=0.1;//first parameter of the Waxman model
second_parameter=0.8;//second parameter of the Waxman model
//1.generation of topology using Waxman mode
display=5;//display parameter
WindowNumber=4;//window index
[TopologyGraph,localityradius]=NL_T_Waxman(first_parameter,
    second_parameter,NumberOfNodes,area);//application of
    NL_T_Waxman
VisualizeNodeEdges=NL_G_ShowGraphN(TopologyGraph,WindowNumber)
    ;//graph visualization
xtitle("generation of topology using Waxman mode");
WindowNumber=5;//window index
scf(WindowNumber);
clf(WindowNumber);
plot(localityradius);
plot2d3(localityradius);//graph visualization
nr=length(TopologyGraph.node_x);//real network size
nl=length(TopologyGraph.head);
i=NL_F_RandInt1n(length(TopologyGraph.node_x));//selection of
    the source node
pred=zeros(1,NumberOfNodes);//initialization
v=[];//visited
c=[];//candidates
[v,c,pred]=NL_R_DFSSearchEnd(i,TopologyGraph,v,c,pred);//
    application of NL_R_DFSSearchEnd
display_candidates=[];//display the candidates, the first ones
    are represented with the smallest edge width
for j=1:length(c)
```

```
display_candidates=[display_candidates NL_G_Nodes2Path([v c(j)
    ],TopologyGraph)];
end
Bdi=5;
Ebi=2;
EdgeColor=ones(1,nl);//edge color
EdgeWidth=Ebi*ones(1,nl);//edge width
EdgeColor(display_candidates)=5;
EdgeWidth(display_candidates)=Ebi*(1:length(display_candidates)
    );
node_border=Bdi*ones(1,nr);//node border
node_border([v c])=2*Bdi;
TopologyGraph.node_border=node_border;
TopologyGraph.edge_color=EdgeColor;
TopologyGraph.edge_width=EdgeWidth;
WindowNumber=6;//window index
[VisualizeNodeEdges]=NL_G_ShowGraphN(TopologyGraph,WindowNumber
    );//graph visualization
xtitle("Generation of dfs_search_end for Waxman mode topology")
    ;
i
v
c
pred


NumberOfNodes=80;//number of nodes
area=1000;//network squared area side
localityradius=100;//Locality radius
first_parameter=0.1;//first parameter of the Waxman model
second_parameter=0.8;//second parameter of the Waxman model
//1.generation of topology using Waxman mode
display=5;//display parameter
WindowNumber=7;//window index
[TopologyGraph,localityradius]=NL_T_Waxman(first_parameter,
    second_parameter,NumberOfNodes,area);//application of
    NL_T_Waxman
VisualizeNodeEdges=NL_G_ShowGraphN(TopologyGraph,WindowNumber)
    ;//graph visualization
xtitle("generation of topology using Waxman mode");
WindowNumber=8;//window index
scf(WindowNumber);
clf(WindowNumber);
plot(localityradius);
plot2d3(localityradius);//graph visualization
nr=length(TopologyGraph.node_x);//real network size
nl=length(TopologyGraph.head);
i=NL_F_RandInt1n(length(TopologyGraph.node_x));//selection of
    the source node
pred=zeros(1,NumberOfNodes);//initialization
```

```
v=[];//visited
c=[];//candidates
[v,c,pred]=NL_R_DFSSearchEnd(i,TopologyGraph,v,c,pred);//
    application of NL_R_DFSSearchEnd
display_candidates=[];//display the candidates, the first ones
    are represented with the smallest edge width
for j=1:length(c)
display_candidates=[display_candidates NL_G_Nodes2Path([v c(j)
    ],TopologyGraph)];
end
Bdi=5;
Ebi=2;
EdgeColor=ones(1,nl);//edge color
EdgeWidth=Ebi*ones(1,nl);//edge width
EdgeColor(display_candidates)=5;
EdgeWidth(display_candidates)=Ebi*(1:length(display_candidates)
    );
node_border=Bdi*ones(1,nr);//node border
node_border([v c])=2*Bdi;
TopologyGraph.node_border=node_border;
TopologyGraph.edge_color=EdgeColor;
TopologyGraph.edge_width=EdgeWidth;
WindowNumber=9;//window index
[VisualizeNodeEdges]=NL_G_ShowGraphN(TopologyGraph,WindowNumber
    );//graph visualization
xtitle("Generation of dfs_search_end for Waxman mode topology")
    ;
i
v
c
pred
```

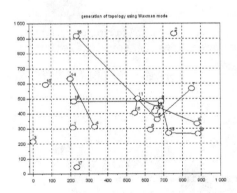
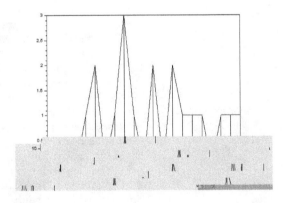

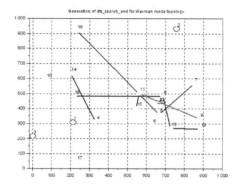

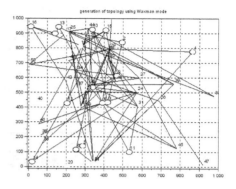

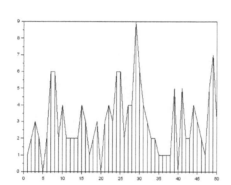

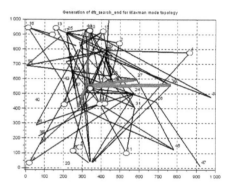

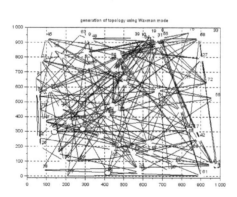

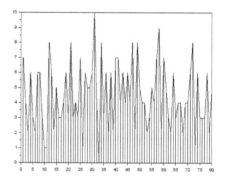

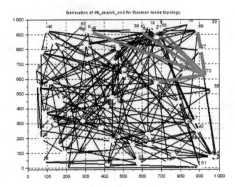

2.11   Generation of AddWaxman to Node topology

```
//This graph is to apply DFS to a random source node and
    display the correspondung graphs
//1.Generation of NL_T_AddWaxman2Node topology
//2.Generation of dfs_search_end for NL_T_AddWaxman2Node
    topology

NumberOfNodes=50;//number of nodes
area=1000;//network squared area side
localityradius=100;//Locality radius
squarearea=1000;//network square area side
dmax=100;//Locality radius
// generation of NL_T_AddWaxman2Node topology
[TopologyGraph]=NL_T_LocalityConnex(NumberOfNodes,area,
    localityradius);//generation of a topology
i=NL_F_RandInt1n(length(TopologyGraph.node_x));//selection of
    the source nodes
nr=length(TopologyGraph.node_x);//real network size
nl=length(TopologyGraph.head);
i=NL_F_RandInt1n(length(TopologyGraph.node_x));//selection of
    the source node
pred=zeros(1,NumberOfNodes);//initialization
v=[];//visited
c=[];//candidates
[v,c,pred]=NL_R_DFSSearchEnd(i,TopologyGraph,v,c,pred);//
    application of NL_R_DFSSearchEnd
display_candidates=[];//display the candidates, the first ones
    are represented with the smallest edge width
for j=1:length(c)
display_candidates=[display_candidates NL_G_Nodes2Path([v c(j)
    ],TopologyGraph)];
end
first_parameter=0.4;//Waxman parameters
second_parameter=0.8;
newN=20;//quantity of nodes of the new subnetwork
newD=150;//maximal radius between new nodes and the central
    node
[ge]=NL_T_AddWaxman2Node(first_parameter,second_parameter,newN,
    newD,TopologyGraph,i);//application of NL_T_AddWaxman2Node
gl=length(TopologyGraph.head);//visualization parameters
gel=length(ge.head);
gn=length(TopologyGraph.node_x);
gen=length(ge.node_x);
ec=5*ones(1,gel);
ec(1:gl)=ones(1,gl);
nc=5*ones(1,gen);
nc(1:gn)=ones(1,gn);
ge.edge_color=ec;
```

```
ge.node_color=nc;
Bdi=5;
Ebi=2;
EdgeColor=ones(1,nl);//edge color
EdgeWidth=Ebi*ones(1,nl);//edge width
EdgeColor(display_candidates)=5;
EdgeWidth(display_candidates)=Ebi*(1:length(display_candidates)
    );
D=Bdi*ones(1,nr);//node border
D([v c])=2*Bdi;
TopologyGraph.node_border=D;
TopologyGraph.edge_color=EdgeColor;
TopologyGraph.edge_width=EdgeWidth;
WindowNumber=1;//window index
[VisualizeNodeEdges]=NL_G_ShowGraphN(TopologyGraph,WindowNumber
    );//graph visualization
xtitle("Generation of NL_T_AddWaxman2Node topology");
WindowNumber=2;//window index
VisualizeNodeEdges=NL_G_ShowGraph(ge,WindowNumber);//graph
    visualization
xtitle("Generation of dfs_search_end for NL_T_AddWaxman2Node
    topology")
i
v
c
pred

NumberOfNodes=80;//number of nodes
area=1000;//network squared area side
localityradius=100;//Locality radius
squarearea=1000;//network square area side
dmax=100;//Locality radius
// generation of NL_T_AddWaxman2Node topology
[TopologyGraph]=NL_T_LocalityConnex(NumberOfNodes,area,
    localityradius);//generation of a topology
i=NL_F_RandInt1n(length(TopologyGraph.node_x));//selection of
    the source nodes
nr=length(TopologyGraph.node_x);//real network size
nl=length(TopologyGraph.head);
i=NL_F_RandInt1n(length(TopologyGraph.node_x));//selection of
    the source node
pred=zeros(1,NumberOfNodes);//initialization
v=[];//visited
c=[];//candidates
[v,c,pred]=NL_R_DFSSearchEnd(i,TopologyGraph,v,c,pred);//
    application of NL_R_DFSSearchEnd
display_candidates=[];//display the candidates, the first ones
    are represented with the smallest edge width
for j=1:length(c)
```

```
display_candidates=[display_candidates NL_G_Nodes2Path([v c(j)
    ],TopologyGraph)];
end
first_parameter=0.4;//Waxman parameters
second_parameter=0.8;
newN=20;//quantity of nodes of the new subnetwork
newD=150;//maximal radius between new nodes and the central
    node
[ge]=NL_T_AddWaxman2Node(first_parameter,second_parameter,newN,
    newD,TopologyGraph,i);//application of NL_T_AddWaxman2Node
gl=length(TopologyGraph.head);//visualization parameters
gel=length(ge.head);
gn=length(TopologyGraph.node_x);
gen=length(ge.node_x);
ec=5*ones(1,gel);
ec(1:gl)=ones(1,gl);
nc=5*ones(1,gen);
nc(1:gn)=ones(1,gn);
ge.edge_color=ec;
ge.node_color=nc;
Bdi=5;
Ebi=2;
EdgeColor=ones(1,nl);//edge color
EdgeWidth=Ebi*ones(1,nl);//edge width
EdgeColor(display_candidates)=5;
EdgeWidth(display_candidates)=Ebi*(1:length(display_candidates)
    );
D=Bdi*ones(1,nr);//node border
D([v c])=2*Bdi;
TopologyGraph.node_border=D;
TopologyGraph.edge_color=EdgeColor;
TopologyGraph.edge_width=EdgeWidth;
WindowNumber=3;//window index
[VisualizeNodeEdges]=NL_G_ShowGraphN(TopologyGraph,WindowNumber
    );//graph visualization
xtitle("Generation of NL_T_AddWaxman2Node topology");
WindowNumber=4;//window index
VisualizeNodeEdges=NL_G_ShowGraph(ge,WindowNumber);//graph
    visualization
xtitle("Generation of dfs_search_end for NL_T_AddWaxman2Node
    topology")
i
v
c
pred


NumberOfNodes=110;//number of nodes
area=1000;//network squared area side
localityradius=100;//Locality radius
```

```
squarearea=1000;//network square area side
dmax=100;//Locality radius
// generation of NL_T_AddWaxman2Node topology
[TopologyGraph]=NL_T_LocalityConnex(NumberOfNodes,area,
    localityradius);//generation of a topology
i=NL_F_RandInt1n(length(TopologyGraph.node_x));//selection of
    the source nodes
nr=length(TopologyGraph.node_x);//real network size
nl=length(TopologyGraph.head);
i=NL_F_RandInt1n(length(TopologyGraph.node_x));//selection of
    the source node
pred=zeros(1,NumberOfNodes);//initialization
v=[];//visited
c=[];//candidates
[v,c,pred]=NL_R_DFSSearchEnd(i,TopologyGraph,v,c,pred);//
    application of NL_R_DFSSearchEnd
display_candidates=[];//display the candidates, the first ones
    are represented with the smallest edge width
for j=1:length(c)
display_candidates=[display_candidates NL_G_Nodes2Path([v c(j)
    ],TopologyGraph)];
end
first_parameter=0.4;//Waxman parameters
second_parameter=0.8;
newN=20;//quantity of nodes of the new subnetwork
newD=150;//maximal radius between new nodes and the central
    node
[ge]=NL_T_AddWaxman2Node(first_parameter,second_parameter,newN,
    newD,TopologyGraph,i);//application of NL_T_AddWaxman2Node
gl=length(TopologyGraph.head);//visualization parameters
gel=length(ge.head);
gn=length(TopologyGraph.node_x);
gen=length(ge.node_x);
ec=5*ones(1,gel);
ec(1:gl)=ones(1,gl);
nc=5*ones(1,gen);
nc(1:gn)=ones(1,gn);
ge.edge_color=ec;
ge.node_color=nc;
Bdi=5;
Ebi=2;
EdgeColor=ones(1,nl);//edge color
EdgeWidth=Ebi*ones(1,nl);//edge width
EdgeColor(display_candidates)=5;
EdgeWidth(display_candidates)=Ebi*(1:length(display_candidates)
    );
D=Bdi*ones(1,nr);//node border
D([v c])=2*Bdi;
TopologyGraph.node_border=D;
TopologyGraph.edge_color=EdgeColor;
```

```
TopologyGraph.edge_width=EdgeWidth;
WindowNumber=5;//window index
[VisualizeNodeEdges]=NL_G_ShowGraphN(TopologyGraph,WindowNumber
    );//graph visualization
xtitle("Generation of NL_T_AddWaxman2Node topology");
WindowNumber=6;//window index
VisualizeNodeEdges=NL_G_ShowGraph(ge,WindowNumber);//graph
    visualization
xtitle("Generation of dfs_search_end for NL_T_AddWaxman2Node
    topology")
i
v
c
pred
```

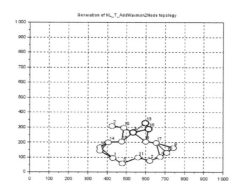
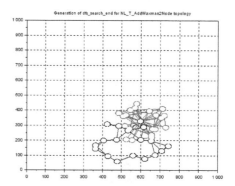
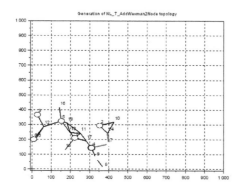
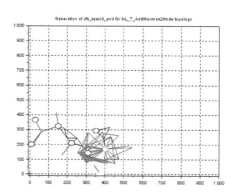

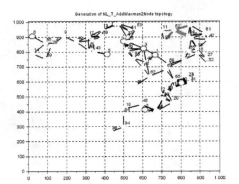
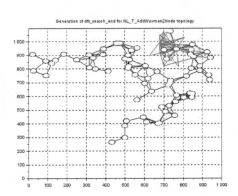

2.12   Generation of waxmann using DFSWeightPlot

```
//This graph is to apply DFSWeightPlot to a random source node
    and display the corresponding graphs.
//Generation of DFSWeightPlot using Waxman Topology with 20
    nodes
//1. Generation of waxmann using DFSWeightPlot
//2 Generation of DFSWeightPlot
```

```
param1=0.2;//first parameter of the Waxman model
param2=0.7;//second parameter of the Waxman model
NumberOfNodes=20;//number of nodes
WaxArea=1000;//network squared area side of NL_T_Waxman
DFSWPArea=1000;//network square area side of DFSWeightPlot
//1. Generation of waxmann using DFSWeightPlot
[TopologyGraph,NodeDiameter]=NL_T_Waxman(param1,param2,
    NumberOfNodes,WaxArea);//application of NL_T_Waxman
WindowNumber=1;//window index
VisualizeNodesEdges=NL_G_ShowGraphN(TopologyGraph,WindowNumber)
    ;//graph visualization
xtitle("Generation of topology in Waxman using DFSWeightPlot
    for 20 nodes","X-Nodes","Y-Nodes");
i=NL_F_RandInt1n(length(TopologyGraph.node_x));//selection of
    the source node
display=2;//display parameter
WindowNumber=2;//window index
//2 Generation of DFSWeightPlot
[go,v,pred]=NL_R_DFSWeightPlot(TopologyGraph,i,display,
    WindowNumber);//application of NL_R_DFSWeightPlot
xtitle("Generation of DFSWeightPlot for 20 nodes","X-Nodes","Y-
    Nodes");
i
v(1:10)//first ten values
pred(1:10)//first ten values
i2=3;//window index
scf(i2);
clf(i2);
plot(NodeDiameter);
plot2d3(NodeDiameter);//graph visualization
xtitle('Graph Visualization for 20 nodes','node index','degree'
    );

//Generation of DFSWeightPlot using Waxman Topology with 70
    nodes
//1. Generation of waxmann using DFSWeightPlot
//2 Generation of DFSWeightPlot

NumberOfNodes=70;//number of nodes
//1. Generation of waxmann using DFSWeightPlot
```

```
[TopologyGraph,NodeDiameter]=NL_T_Waxman(param1,param2,
    NumberOfNodes,WaxArea);//application of NL_T_Waxman
WindowNumber=4;//window index
VisualizeNodesEdges=NL_G_ShowGraphN(TopologyGraph,WindowNumber)
    ;//graph visualization
xtitle("Generation of topology in Waxman using DFSWeightPlot
    for 70 nodes","X-Nodes","Y-Nodes");
i=NL_F_RandInt1n(length(TopologyGraph.node_x));//selection of
    the source node
display=2;//display parameter
WindowNumber=5;//window index
//2 Generation of DFSWeightPlot
[go,v,pred]=NL_R_DFSWeightPlot(TopologyGraph,i,display,
    WindowNumber);//application of NL_R_DFSWeightPlot
xtitle("Generation of DFSWeightPlot for 70 nodes","X-Nodes","Y-
    Nodes");
i
v(1:10)//first ten values
pred(1:10)//first ten values
i2=6;//window index
scf(i2);
clf(i2);
plot(NodeDiameter);
plot2d3(NodeDiameter);//graph visualization
xtitle('Graph Visualization for 70 nodes','node index','degree'
    );


//Generation of DFSWeightPlot using Waxman Topology with 120
    nodes
//1. Generation of waxmann using DFSWeightPlot
//2 Generation of DFSWeightPlot

NumberOfNodes=120;//number of nodes
//1. Generation of waxmann using DFSWeightPlot
[TopologyGraph,NodeDiameter]=NL_T_Waxman(param1,param2,
    NumberOfNodes,WaxArea);//application of NL_T_Waxman
WindowNumber=7;//window index
VisualizeNodesEdges=NL_G_ShowGraphN(TopologyGraph,WindowNumber)
    ;//graph visualization
xtitle("Generation of topology in Waxman using DFSWeightPlot
    for 70 nodes","X-Nodes","Y-Nodes");
i=NL_F_RandInt1n(length(TopologyGraph.node_x));//selection of
    the source node
display=2;//display parameter
WindowNumber=8;//window index
//2 Generation of DFSWeightPlot
[go,v,pred]=NL_R_DFSWeightPlot(TopologyGraph,i,display,
    WindowNumber);//application of NL_R_DFSWeightPlot
xtitle("Generation of DFSWeightPlot for 120 nodes","X-Nodes","Y
    -Nodes");
```

```
i
v(1:20)//first ten values
pred(1:20)//first ten values
i2=9;//window index
scf(i2);
clf(i2);
plot(NodeDiameter);
plot2d3(NodeDiameter);//graph visualization
xtitle('Graph Visualization for 120 nodes','node index','degree
    ');
```

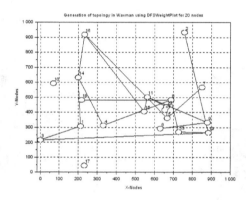

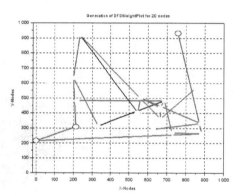

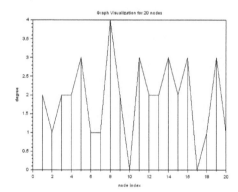

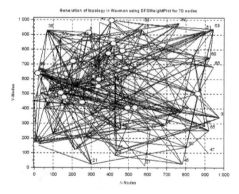

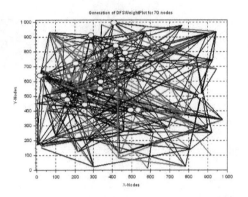

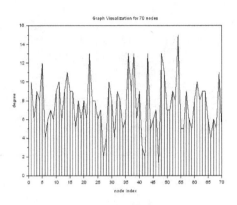

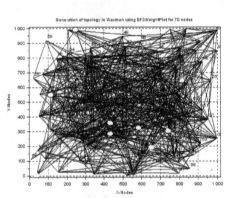

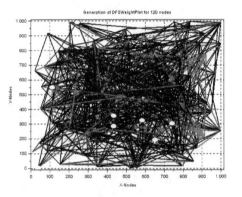

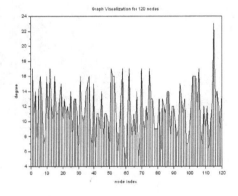

2.13   Generation of DFSWeightPlot for Grid Topology

```
//This graph is to apply DFS to a random source node and
    display the corresponding graphs.
//1. Generation of Locality Connex
//2. Generation of DFSWeightPlot for Grid Topology

//Generation of DFSWeight for NL_T_AddWaxman2Node Topology for
    10 nodes
NumberOfNodes=10;//number of nodes
NetworkArea=1000;//network square area side
LocalityRadius=100;//Locality radius
NumberOfLines=3;//number of lines
NumberOfColumns=5;//number of columns
NetworkArea_x=1000;//network area x-side
NetworkArea_y=1000;//network area x-side
// 1 Generation of Locality Connex
[TopologyGraph]=NL_T_LocalityConnex(NumberOfNodes,NetworkArea,
    LocalityRadius);//generation of a topology in respect with
    the Locality method
[TopologyGraph]=NL_T_Grid(NumberOfLines,NumberOfColumns,
    NetworkArea_x,NetworkArea_y);//application of NL_T_Grid
i=NL_F_RandInt1n(length(TopologyGraph.node_x));//selection of
    the source node
// 2. Generation of DFSWeightPlot for Grid Topology
display=2;//display parameter
WindowNumber=1;//window index
[go,v,pred]=NL_R_DFSWeightPlot(TopologyGraph,i,display,
    WindowNumber);//application of NL_R_DFSWeightPlot
xtitle("Generation of DFSWeightPlot for 10 nodes","X-Nodes","Y-
    Nodes");
NL_G_ShowGraphNE(TopologyGraph,2);//graph visualization
xtitle("Generation of topology in Grid using DFSWeightPlot for
    10 nodes","X-Nodes","Y-Nodes");
i
v(1:10)//first ten values
pred(1:10)//first ten values

//1. Generation of Locality Connex
//2. Generation of DFSWeightPlot for Grid Topology

//Generation of DFSWeight for NL_T_AddWaxman2Node Topology for
    50 nodes
NumberOfNodes=50;//number of nodes
NumberOfLines=5;//number of lines
NumberOfColumns=7;//number of columns
// 1. Generation of Locality Connex
[TopologyGraph]=NL_T_LocalityConnex(NumberOfNodes,NetworkArea,
    LocalityRadius);//generation of a topology in respect with
```

```
    the Locality method
[TopologyGraph]=NL_T_Grid(NumberOfLines,NumberOfColumns,
    NetworkArea_x,NetworkArea_y);//application of NL_T_Grid
i=NL_F_RandInt1n(length(TopologyGraph.node_x));//selection of
    the source node
// 2. Generation of DFSWeightPlot for Grid Topology
display=2;//display parameter
WindowNumber=3;//window index
[go,v,pred]=NL_R_DFSWeightPlot(TopologyGraph,i,display,
    WindowNumber);//application of NL_R_DFSWeightPlot
xtitle("Generation of DFSWeightPlot for 50 nodes","X-Nodes","Y-
    Nodes");
NL_G_ShowGraphNE(TopologyGraph,4);//graph visualization
xtitle("Generation of topology in Grid using DFSWeightPlot for
    50 nodes","X-Nodes","Y-Nodes");
i
v(1:10)//first ten values
pred(1:10)//first ten values


//1. Generation of Locality Connex
//2. Generation of DFSWeightPlot for Grid Topology

//Generation of DFSWeight for NL_T_AddWaxman2Node Topology for
    100 nodes
NumberOfNodes=100;//number of nodes
NumberOfLines=7;//number of lines
NumberOfColumns=9;//number of columns
// 1. Generation of Locality Connex
[TopologyGraph]=NL_T_LocalityConnex(NumberOfNodes,NetworkArea,
    LocalityRadius);//generation of a topology in respect with
    the Locality method
[TopologyGraph]=NL_T_Grid(NumberOfLines,NumberOfColumns,
    NetworkArea_x,NetworkArea_y);//application of NL_T_Grid
i=NL_F_RandInt1n(length(TopologyGraph.node_x));//selection of
    the source node
// 2. Generation of DFSWeightPlot for Grid Topology
display=2;//display parameter
WindowNumber=5;//window index
[go,v,pred]=NL_R_DFSWeightPlot(TopologyGraph,i,display,
    WindowNumber);//application of NL_R_DFSWeightPlot
xtitle("Generation of DFSWeightPlot for 100 nodes","X-Nodes","Y
    -Nodes");
NL_G_ShowGraphNE(TopologyGraph,6);//graph visualization
xtitle("Generation of topology in Grid using DFSWeightPlot for
    100 nodes","X-Nodes","Y-Nodes");
i
v(1:10)//first ten values
pred(1:10)//first ten values
```

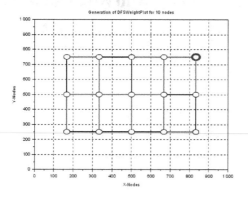

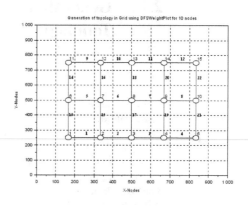

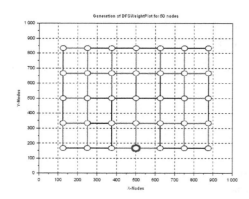

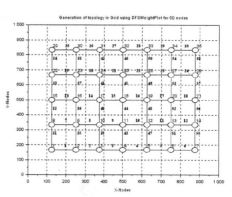

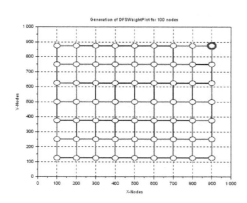

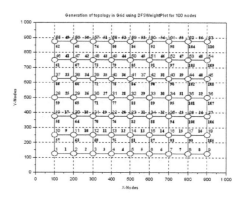

2.14 Generation of DFSWeight for AddWaxman to Node Topology

```
//This graph is to apply DFS to a random source node and
    display the corresponding graphs.
//1. Generation of Locality Connex
//2. Generation of DFSWeight for NL_T_AddWaxman2Node Topology


//Generation of DFSWeight for NL_T_AddWaxman2Node Topology for
    80 nodes
NumberOfNodes=80;// number of nodes
NetworkArea=1000;//network square area side
LocalityRadius=100;//Locality radius
[TopologyGraph]=NL_T_LocalityConnex(NumberOfNodes,NetworkArea,
    LocalityRadius);//generation of a topology in respect with
    the Locality method
i=NL_F_RandInt1n(length(TopologyGraph.node_x));//selection of
    the source node
param1=0.4;//Waxman parameters
param2=0.8;
newN=20;//quantity of nodes of the new subnetwork
newD=150;//maximal radius between new nodes and the central
    node
display=2;//display parameter
[ge]=NL_T_AddWaxman2Node(param1,param2,newN,newD,TopologyGraph,
    i);//application of NL_T_AddWaxman2Node
gl=length(TopologyGraph.head);//visualization parameters
gel=length(ge.head);
gn=length(TopologyGraph.node_x);
gen=length(ge.node_x);
ec=5*ones(1,gel);
ec(1:gl)=ones(1,gl);
nc=5*ones(1,gen);
nc(1:gn)=ones(1,gn);
ge.edge_color=ec;
ge.node_color=nc;
WindowNumber=1;//window index
VisualizeNodesEdges=NL_G_ShowGraphE(ge,WindowNumber);//graph
    visualization
xtitle("Generation of topology in AddWaxman2Node using
    DFSWeightPlot for 80 nodes","X-Nodes","Y-Nodes");
[v,pred]=NL_R_DFSWeight(TopologyGraph,i);//application of
    NL_R_DFSWeight
i
v(1:10)//first ten values
pred(1:10)//first ten values
```

```
//Generation of DFSWeight for NL_T_AddWaxman2Node Topology for
    120 nodes
NumberOfNodes=120;// number of nodes
[TopologyGraph]=NL_T_LocalityConnex(NumberOfNodes,NetworkArea,
    LocalityRadius);//generation of a topology in respect with
    the Locality method
i=NL_F_RandInt1n(length(TopologyGraph.node_x));//selection of
    the source node
param1=0.4;//Waxman parameters
param2=0.8;
newN=20;//quantity of nodes of the new subnetwork
newD=150;//maximal radius between new nodes and the central
    node
display=2;//display parameter
[ge]=NL_T_AddWaxman2Node(param1,param2,newN,newD,TopologyGraph,
    i);//application of NL_T_AddWaxman2Node
gl=length(TopologyGraph.head);//visualization parameters
gel=length(ge.head);
gn=length(TopologyGraph.node_x);
gen=length(ge.node_x);
ec=5*ones(1,gel);
ec(1:gl)=ones(1,gl);
nc=5*ones(1,gen);
nc(1:gn)=ones(1,gn);
ge.edge_color=ec;
ge.node_color=nc;
WindowNumber=2;//window index
VisualizeNodesEdges=NL_G_ShowGraphE(ge,WindowNumber);//graph
    visualization
xtitle("Generation of topology in AddWaxman2Node using
    DFSWeightPlot for 120 nodes","X-Nodes","Y-Nodes");
[v,pred]=NL_R_DFSWeight(TopologyGraph,i);//application of
    NL_R_DFSWeight
i
v(1:10)//first ten values
pred(1:10)//first ten values


//Generation of DFSWeight for NL_T_AddWaxman2Node Topology for
    160 nodes
NumberOfNodes=160;// number of nodes
[TopologyGraph]=NL_T_LocalityConnex(NumberOfNodes,NetworkArea,
    LocalityRadius);//generation of a topology in respect with
    the Locality method
i=NL_F_RandInt1n(length(TopologyGraph.node_x));//selection of
    the source node
param1=0.4;//Waxman parameters
param2=0.8;
newN=20;//quantity of nodes of the new subnetwork
newD=150;//maximal radius between new nodes and the central
    node
```

```
display=2;//display parameter
[ge]=NL_T_AddWaxman2Node(param1,param2,newN,newD,TopologyGraph,
    i);//application of NL_T_AddWaxman2Node
gl=length(TopologyGraph.head);//visualization parameters
gel=length(ge.head);
gn=length(TopologyGraph.node_x);
gen=length(ge.node_x);
ec=5*ones(1,gel);
ec(1:gl)=ones(1,gl);
nc=5*ones(1,gen);
nc(1:gn)=ones(1,gn);
ge.edge_color=ec;
ge.node_color=nc;
WindowNumber=3;//window index
VisualizeNodesEdges=NL_G_ShowGraphE(ge,WindowNumber);//graph
    visualization
xtitle("Generation of topology in AddWaxman2Node using
    DFSWeightPlot for 160 nodes","X-Nodes","Y-Nodes");
[v,pred]=NL_R_DFSWeight(TopologyGraph,i);//application of
    NL_R_DFSWeight
i
v(1:10)//first ten values
pred(1:10)//first ten values
```

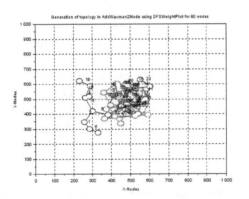
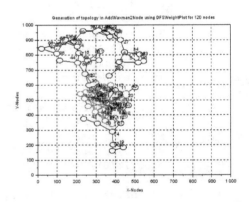

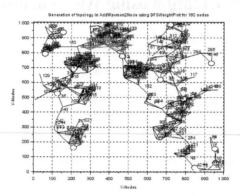

Generation of topology in AddWaxman2Node using DFSWeightPlot for 160 nodes

2.15   Nertwork Topology Creation using Waxman layer approach

```
a=[0.3 0.3 0.3 0.3];//first parameter of the Waxman model for
    each network layer
b=[0.9 0.7 0.5 0.3];//second parameter of the Waxman model for
    each network layer
nl=[30 50 50 100];//quantity of nodes per network layer
l=[1000 150 100 40];//squared area side per network layer
n=[3 5 3 3];//maximal quantity of nodes per subnetwork for each
    layer
s=4;//quantity of network layers
db=20;//original diameter of nodes
dd=5;//diameter difference between successive network layers
cv=[2 5 6 1];//color of each network layer
[g,d,nl]=Ntg(a,b,nl,l,n,s,db,dd,cv);//application of Ntg
nf=length(g.node_x);//real network size
nl=length(g.head);//quantity of network links
[i,j]=Random_i_j(nf);//selection of the extremal nodes
[path]=RoutingDijkstra(g,'arc',i,j);//application of
    RoutingDijkstra
p=nodes_2_path(path,g);
EC=ones(1,nl);//display the path between i and j
EB=ones(1,nl);
EC(p)=5;
EB(p)=2;
D=ones(1,nf);
D(path)=3;
g.node_border=D;
g.edge_color=EC;
g.edge_width=EB;
show_graph(g);
```

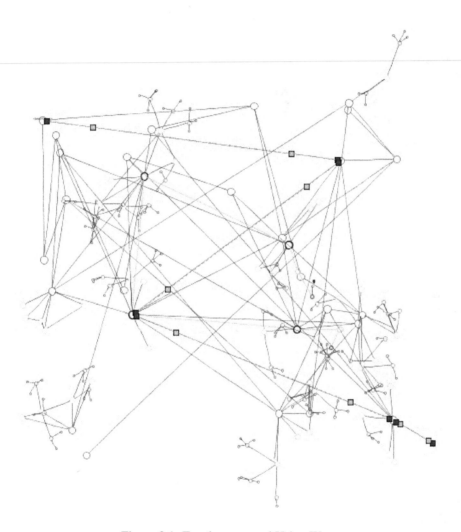

Figure 2.1: Topology created Using Waxman

2.16   Application of Routing FloydWarshall

```
n=100;//network size
l=1000;//network squared area side
d=100;//Locality radius
[g]=NtgLocalityConnex(n,l,d);//generation of a topology
nr=length(g.node_x);//real network size
nl=length(g.head);
i=Random(length(g.node_x));//selection of the source node
pred=zeros(1,n);//initialization
v=[];//visited
c=[];//candidates
[v,c,pred]=RoutingSearchDistance(i,g,v,c,pred);//application of
     RoutingSearchDistance
p=[];//display the candidates, the first ones are represented
    with the smallest edge width
for i=1:length(c)
p=[p nodes_2_path([v c(i)],g)]
end
EC=ones(1,nl);
EB=ones(1,nl);
EC(p)=5;
D=ones(1,nr);
D([v c])=3;
g.node_border=D;
g.edge_color=EC;
g.edge_width=EB;
show_graph(g);
i
v
c
pred
load('./demos/RoutingTables_topo_100_1.dat');//loading of the
    network routing tables
g=load_graph('./demos/topo_100_1.graph');//loading of the
    network graph
[g]=EdgeLength(g);
[Path,Next]=RoutingFloydWarshall(g);//Application of
    RoutingFloydWarshall
Path(1:10,1:10)
Next(1:10,1:10)
```

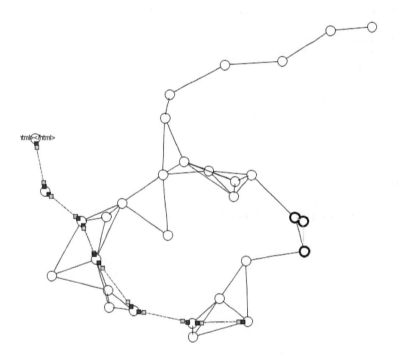

Figure 2.2: Application Of Routing Using Floydwarshall

2.17 Application of BellmanFord

```
n=80;//network size
L=1000;//network square area side
dmax=100;//locality radius
[g]=NL_T_LocalityConnex(n,L,dmax);//generation of a random
    topology in respect with the Locality method.
i=NL_F_RandInt1n(length(g.node_x));//selection of the source
    node
[g]=NL_T_LocalityConnex(n,L,dmax);//generation of a topology in
    respect with the Locality method
i=NL_F_RandInt1n(length(g.node_x));//selection of the source
    node
dw=2;//display parameter
ind=1;//window index
[go,v,pred]=NL_R_DFSPlot(g,i,dw,ind);//application of
    NL_R_DFSPlot
EB=5*ones(1,length(g.node_x));//display the source node: border
EC=ones(1,length(g.node_x));//color
EB(i)=10;
EC(i)=5;
g.node_border=EB;
g.node_color=EC;
ind=1;//window index
f=NL_G_ShowGraphN(g,ind);//graph visualization
[dist,pred]=NL_R_BellmanFord(g,i);//application of
    NL_R_BellmanFord
i
dist(1:10)//first ten nodes
pred//first ten nodes
```

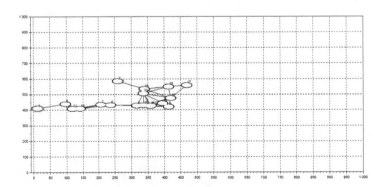

Figure 2.3: Bellmanford Application

2.18   Application of Dijkstra

```
n=80;//network size
L=1000;//network square area side
dmax=100;//locality radius
[g]=NL_T_LocalityConnex(n,L,dmax);//generation of a random
    topology in respect with the Locality method.
i=NL_F_RandInt1n(length(g.node_x));//selection of the source
    node
ind=1;//window index
g.node_diam(i)=40;//node diameter
g.node_border(i)=10;//node border
g.node_color(i)=5;//node color
[f]=NL_G_ShowGraphN(g,ind);//graph visualization
[dist,pred]=NL_R_Dijkstra(g,i);//application of NL_R_Dijkstra
i
dist(1:10)//first ten values
pred(1:10)//first ten values
```

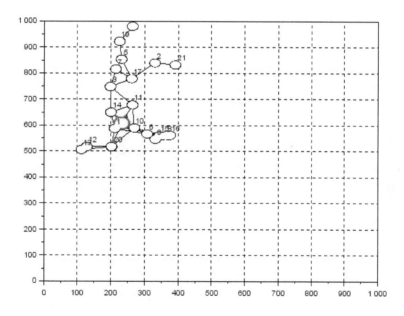

Figure 2.4: Dijikstra Application

2.19   DFS Weight Plot

```
n=150;//network size
L=1000;//network square area side
dmax=100;//Locality radius
[g]=NL_T_LocalityConnex(n,L,dmax);//generation of a topology in
    respect with the Locality method
i=NL_F_RandInt1n(length(g.node_x));//selection of the source
    node
//i=NL_F_RandInt1n(length(g.node_x))//selection of the source
    node
pred=zeros(1,n);//initialization
v=[];//visited
c=[];//candidates
[v,c,pred]=NL_R_PrimSearchDistance(i,g,v,c,pred)//application
    of NL_R_PrimSearchDistance
dw=2;//display parameter
ind=1;//window index
[go,v,pred]=NL_R_DFSWeightPlot(g,i,dw,ind);//application of
    NL_R_DFSWeightPlot
//i
//v(1:10)//first ten values
//pred(1:10)//first ten values
```

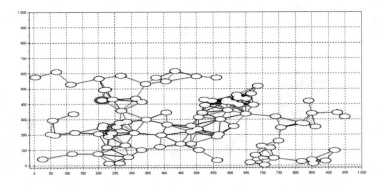

Figure 2.5: Weight of DFS

2.20   Application of Prims

```
n=150;//network size
L=1000;//network square area side
dmax=100;//Locality radius
[g]=NL_T_LocalityConnex(n,L,dmax);//generation of a topology in
    respect with the Locality method
i=NL_F_RandInt1n(length(g.node_x));//selection of the source
    node
//for i=1:edge_number(g), hilite_edges(i);xpause(3d5);
    unhilite_edges(i), end;
//hilite_edges(1:3:edge_number(g))
dw=2;//display parameter
ind=1;//window index
[go,v,pred]=NL_R_Prim(g,i,dw,ind)//application of NL_R_Prim
for i=1:edge_number(g), hilite_edges(i);xpause(3d5);
    unhilite_edges(i), end;
hilite_edges(1:4:edge_number(g))
```

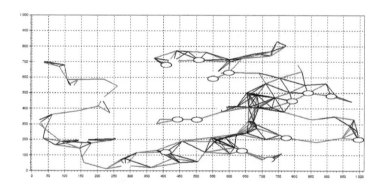

Figure 2.6: Prims Application

2.21 One node to the closest Access Point in respect with multiple paths.

```
n=100;
cr=120;
L=1000;
r=10;//display radius of moving nodes
rf=15;//display radius of fixed nodes
rs=20;//display radius of the moving nodes belonging to the
    connection under studies
nf=5;//quantity of fixed nodes
Tlim=100;//simulation duration
Tmax=100;//maximal waiting time
dmax=180;//Locality radius for the links attribution
ind=1;//window index

nx=L*rand(1,n);//current x-coordinate of all nodes
ny=L*rand(1,n);//current y-coordinate of all nodes
//n=3;
//cr=250;
//nx=[100 200 300];
//ny=[100 300 100];
name='NL_M_Simulation1N2CAPMP';
t=[];
h=[];
[g]=NL_G_MakeGraph(name,n,t,h,nx,ny);//creation of a network
    graph
[h,t]=NL_M_Locality(g.node_x,g.node_y,cr);//application of
    NL_M_Locality
g.head=h;
g.tail=t;
i=1;//window index
f=NL_M_Background(i,name);//application of NL_M_Background
r=10;//radius
c=1;//color
t=0;
f=NL_M_GraphDisplayUpdate(g,i,r,c);
vm=10;
v=vm*rand(1,n);//velocity for each node
a=2*%pi*rand(1,n);//angle for each node
for i=1:200
    [g,f,a]=NL_M_GraphRD(g,f,v,a,cr);//application of
        NL_M_GraphRD
end
NL_M_Simulation1N2CAPMP(r,rf,rs,n,nf,L,vm,Tlim,Tmax,dmax,ind)
    ;//Application of NL_M_Simulation1N2CAPMP
```

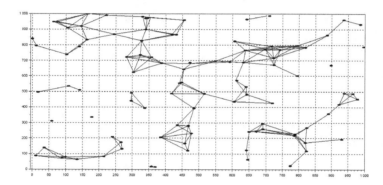

Figure 2.7: Finding Best Access Point over Multiple Access Point

2.22   One node towards the closest Access Points

```
n=100;
cr=120;
L=1000;
r=10;//display radius of moving nodes
rf=15;//display radius of fixed nodes
rs=20;//display radius of the moving nodes belonging to the
    connection under studies
nf=5;//quantity of fixed nodes
Tlim=100;//simulation duration
Tmax=100;//maximal waiting time
dmax=180;//Locality radius for the links attribution
ind=1;//window index

nx=L*rand(1,n);//current x-coordinate of all nodes
ny=L*rand(1,n);//current y-coordinate of all nodes
//n=3;
//cr=250;
//nx=[100 200 300];
//ny=[100 300 100];
name='NL_M_Simulation1N2CAP(';
t=[];
h=[];
[g]=NL_G_MakeGraph(name,n,t,h,nx,ny);//creation of a network
    graph
[h,t]=NL_M_Locality(g.node_x,g.node_y,cr);//application of
    NL_M_Locality
g.head=h;
g.tail=t;
i=1;//window index
f=NL_M_Background(i,name);//application of NL_M_Background
r=10;//radius
c=3;//color
t=0;
f=NL_M_GraphDisplayUpdate(g,i,r,c);
vm=10;
v=vm*rand(1,n);//velocity for each node
a=2*%pi*rand(1,n);//angle for each node
for i=1:200
    [g,f,a]=NL_M_GraphRD(g,f,v,a,cr);//application of
        NL_M_GraphRD
end
NL_M_Simulation1N2CAP(r,rf,rs,n,nf,L,vm,Tlim,Tmax,dmax,ind);//
    application of NL_M_Simulation1N2CAP
```

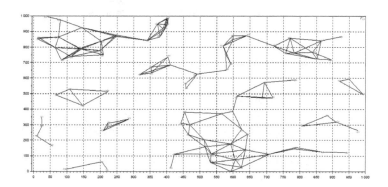

Figure 2.8: One node towards the closest Access Points

2.23   One node towards all reachable Access Points

```
n=100;
cr=120;
L=1000;
r=10;//display radius of moving nodes
rf=15;//display radius of fixed nodes
rs=20;//display radius of the moving nodes belonging to the
     connection under studies
nf=5;//quantity of fixed nodes
Tlim=100;//simulation duration
Tmax=100;//maximal waiting time
dmax=180;//Locality radius for the links attribution
ind=1;//window index

nx=L*rand(1,n);//current x-coordinate of all nodes
ny=L*rand(1,n);//current y-coordinate of all nodes
//n=3;
//cr=250;
//nx=[100 200 300];
//ny=[100 300 100];
name='NL_M_Simulation1N2AllAP';
t=[];
h=[];
[g]=NL_G_MakeGraph(name,n,t,h,nx,ny);//creation of a network
     graph
[h,t]=NL_M_Locality(g.node_x,g.node_y,cr);//application of
     NL_M_Locality
g.head=h;
g.tail=t;
i=1;//window index
f=NL_M_Background(i,name);//application of NL_M_Background
r=10;//radius
c=1;//color
t=0;
f=NL_M_GraphDisplayUpdate(g,i,r,c);
vm=10;
v=vm*rand(1,n);//velocity for each node
a=2*%pi*rand(1,n);//angle for each node
for i=1:200
    [g,f,a]=NL_M_GraphRD(g,f,v,a,cr);//application of
        NL_M_GraphRD
end
NL_M_Simulation1N2AllAP(r,rf,rs,n,nf,L,vm,Tlim,Tmax,dmax,ind)
     ;//application of NL_M_Simulation1N2AllAP
```

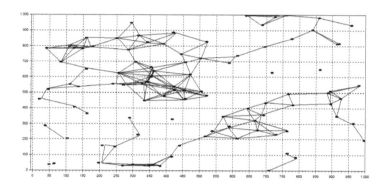

Figure 2.9: One node towards all reachable Access Points

2.24 Topology Creation and application of Routing Dijkstra

```
networksize=150;//network size

areaside=1000;//network squared area side

Localityradius=60;//Locality radius

[TopologyGraph]=NtgLocalityConnex(networksize,areaside,
    Localityradius);//generation of a topology

//show_graph(TopologyGraph);

quantityofsources=2;//quantity of sources

[s,t,tn]=TopologyRecDijkstraNS(TopologyGraph,quantityofsources)
    ;//application of TopologyRecDijkstraNS
s
t
tn

networksize=length(TopologyGraph.node_x);//real network size

networklength=length(TopologyGraph.head);//quantity of network
    links

[i,j]=Random_i_j(networksize);//selection of the extremal nodes
i
j

[path_dis]=RoutingDijkstra(TopologyGraph,'arc',i,j);//
    application of RoutingDijkstra

p=nodes_2_path(path_dis,TopologyGraph);
EC=ones(1,networklength);//display the path between i and j

EB=ones(1,networklength);

EC(p)=5;

EB(p)=2;

D=ones(1,networksize);

D(path_dis)=3;

TopologyGraph.node_border=D;
```

```
TopologyGraph.edge_color=EC;

TopologyGraph.edge_width=EB;

show_graph(TopologyGraph);

path_dis
```

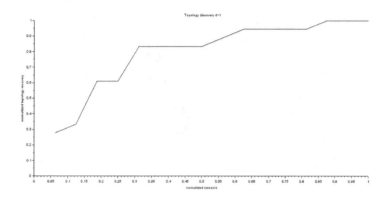

Figure 2.10: Topology Creation and application of Routing Dijkstra

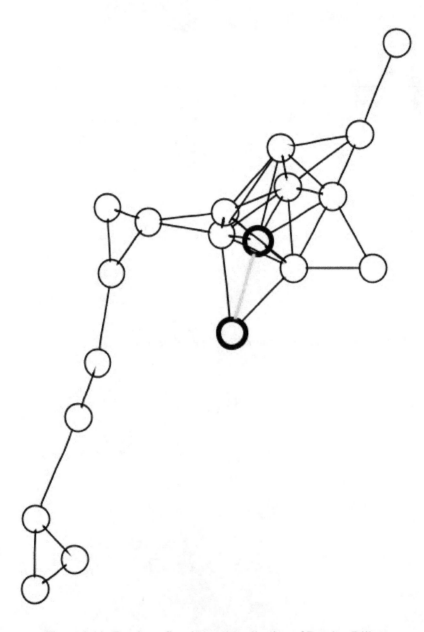

Figure 2.11: Topology Creation and application of Routing Dijkstra

2.25   BellmanFord Shortest Path

```
//Scilab Code for Bellman Ford Algorithm

//The BellmanFord algorithm is an algorithm that computes
    shortest paths from a single source vertex to all of the
    other vertices in a weighted digraph. It is slower than
    Dijkstra's algorithm for the same problem, but more
    versatile, as it is capable of handling graphs in which some
    of the edge weights are negative numbers.



clc;
clear;

//this function works like BELLMAN FORD which takes 4 arguments
function minRoute(graphInFormOfMatrix,resultArray,numVertice,
    node)

    //k is used to repeat the process numVertice times
    for k = 1 : numVertice

        //this nested loop is used to parse the 2D array
        for row = 1:numVertice

            count = row ;

            for col = 1:numVertice

                if(graphInFormOfMatrix(count) == %inf ) then
                    // Do nothing here because vertice/node are not
                        joint with this vertice/node

                else if(graphInFormOfMatrix(count) == 0) then
                    //Do nothing here because self traversal is
                        minimum distance only

                else
                    //Checking whether shortest path is present in
                        result or not
                    x= resultArray(row)+graphInFormOfMatrix(count);
                    y= resultArray(col);

                    //If shortest path is not present, then it will
                        be overwritten below
                    if x < y then

                        //modify the result array
```

```
                    resultArray(col) = x ;

            end

        end

        end

        count = count + numVertice;

      end
    end
  end

//displaying the output
printf("Shortest Path Array %s",node);
disp (resultArray);

endfunction;


//----------------------------------------------------------------------------


//Draw any graph of your choice
//and then convert it into matrix, graph (below)
graphInFormOfMatrix = [0 1 %inf %inf %inf; 1 0 %inf %inf %inf;
    %inf %inf 0 7 %inf; 2 %inf %inf 0 7 ; %inf 3 %inf %inf 0];

//write the number of vertices in graph below
numVertice = 5 ;

//write the number of edges in the graph below
numEdge = 6 ;

//----------------------------------------------------------------------------


//Place 0 at that node number whose shortest distance from all
    other node you wnat to calculate
//and place all other as Infinty
//Then just call the function minRoute


//example 1
//here minimum distance from node A has to be calculated
//so 1st index is placed 0
//and all other indexes are kept Infinty
nodeA = [0 %inf %inf %inf %inf ];
node = "A";
```

```
//Now just call the function minRoute with appropriate
    arguments
//this function works like BELLMAN FORD which takes 4 arguments
minRoute(graphInFormOfMatrix,nodeA,numVertice,node);


//example 2
nodeB = [%inf 0 %inf %inf %inf ];
node = "B";
//this function works like BELLMAN FORD which takes 4 arguments
minRoute(graphInFormOfMatrix,nodeB,numVertice,node);


//example 3
nodeC = [%inf %inf 0 %inf %inf ];
node = "C";
//this function works like BELLMAN FORD which takes 4 arguments
minRoute(graphInFormOfMatrix,nodeC,numVertice,node);


//example 4
nodeD = [%inf %inf %inf 0 %inf ];
node = "D";
//this function works like BELLMAN FORD which takes 4 arguments
minRoute(graphInFormOfMatrix,nodeD,numVertice,node);


//example 5
nodeE = [%inf %inf %inf %inf 0];
node = "E";
//this function works like BELLMAN FORD which takes 4 arguments
minRoute(graphInFormOfMatrix,nodeE,numVertice,node);
```

Output

```
 Shortest Path Array A
   0.   1.   Inf   Inf   Inf
 Shortest Path Array B
   1.   0.   Inf   Inf   Inf
 Shortest Path Array C
   9.   10.   0.   7.   14.
 Shortest Path Array D
   2.   3.   Inf   0.   7.
 Shortest Path Array E
   4.   3.   Inf   Inf   0.
```

2.26 Comparison of Dijktras and Prims

```
n=150;//network size
L=1000;//network square area side
dmax=100;//Locality radius
//generation of a topology in respect with the Locality method
[g]=NtgLocalityConnex(n,L,dmax);
/////Djkstrs Routing Algorithm
nf=length(g.node_x);//real network size
nl=length(g.head);//quantity of network links
[i,j]=Random_i_j(nf);//selection of the extremal nodes
[path]=RoutingDijkstra(g,'arc',i,j);//application of
    RoutingDijkstra
p=nodes_2_path(path,g);
EC=ones(1,nl);//display the path between i and j
EB=ones(1,nl);
EC(p)=5;
EB(p)=2;
D=ones(1,nf);
D(path)=3;
g.node_border=D;
g.edge_color=EC;
g.edge_width=EB;
show_graph(g);
path
//////////Prims Algorithm Performed in the Same Graph
    ///////////////
dmax=100;//Locality radius
i=Random(length(g.node_x));//selection of the source node
dw=2;//display parameter
[v,pred]=RoutingPrim(g,i,dw);//application of RoutingPrim
v
pred
```

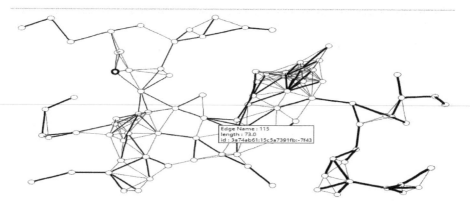

Figure 2.12: BFS

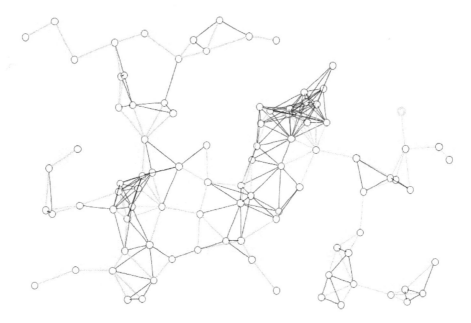

Figure 2.13: DFS

2.27 Edge Length of Nodes

```
n=50;//network size
L=1000;//network square area side
dmax=100;//locality radius
[g]=NtgLocalityConnex(n,L,dmax);//generation of a random
    topology in respect with the Locality method.
show_graph(g);
g.edges.data.length=[]
[g]=EdgeLength(g);//application of EdgeLength
g.edges.data.length
```

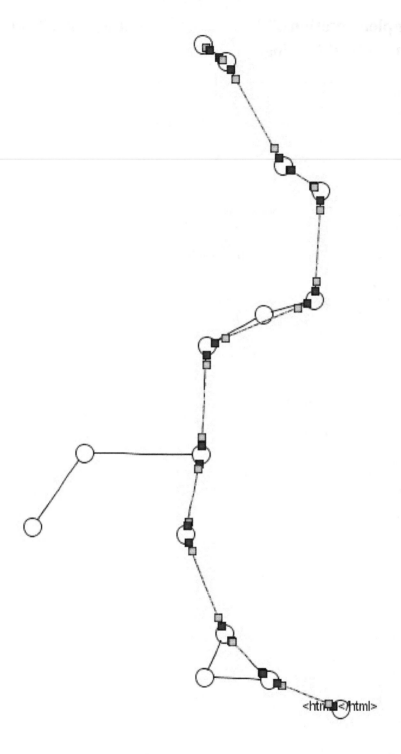

Figure 2.14: Edge Length of Nodes

2.28 Implementation of floyd warshall routing algorithm for differnt topologies

```
//Implementation of floyd warshall routing algorithm for
    differnt topologies
//This code is made by Sagar Thakare Computer Science student
    at VIT uiversity Chennai
clc ;
clear ;
funcprot (0)
//here FLOYD WARSHALL algorithm is implemented
function [ path ]= flyodwarshall(mat ,n)


    //printing Initial state of the graph using matrix
   printf("\nInitial State of the graph\n");

    //this nested loop is used to parse the 2D array
    //to parse the row of array
    for i=1: n

       //to parse the columns of array
       for j=1: n

          if(mat((i -1)*n+j)==%inf)
             printf("\nThere is not direct edge between %d and %
                d",i,j);
             else
           printf("\nThe distance of Vertex %d to Vertex %d is %d
              ",i,j,mat ((i -1)*n+j));
          end
       end
       printf("\n");
    end
      //printing Initial matrix
    printf("\nMatrix formed is\n");
   // this nested loop is used to parse the array
   //and finally print them using printf function in scilab
   for i=1: n
      for j=1: n
         printf(" %d ",mat ((i -1)*n+j));
      end
      printf("\n");
   end


    //floyd warshall algorithm
    for i =1: n
```

```
    for j =1: n
   path ((i -1)*n+j)=mat((i -1) *n+j);
    end
 end

 //for implementing the process n number of times
 for k =1: n
    // this nested loop is used to parse the array
    for i =1: n
       for j =1: n
          if( (path ((i -1) *n+k) + path((k -1)*n+j)) <
             path((i-1)*n+j))
           path((i -1)*n+j)=path ((i -1) *n+k) + path((k
              -1)*n+j);
         end
       end
    end
 end

 //printing shortest path between two vertices
 printf("
    ------------------------------------------------------------
   ");
 printf ("\n\nShortest Path between the vertices\n\n");

 // this nested loop is used to parse the array
 for i =1: n
   for j =1: n
     printf ("Shortest Path from Vertex %d to Vertex %d is %d\
        n" ,i,j, path ((i -1)*n+j));
   end
 end
 //printing shortest path matrix
 printf("\nShortest path Matrix formed is\n");
 // this nested loop is used to parse the array

 for i=1: n
   for j=1: n
      printf(" %d ",path ((i -1)*n+j));
   end
   printf("\n");
  end
   printf("
    ------------------------------------------------------------
     ");

endfunction
printf("For Tree topology");

n=3;
```

```
mat=[0 1 4 2 0 %inf 3 %inf 0]
path=flyodwarshall(mat ,n)

printf("For Bus topology");

n=3;
mat=[0 1 2 1 0 1 2 1 0]
path=flyodwarshall(mat ,n)
```

Output

```
 For Tree topology
Initial State of the graph

The distance of Vertex 1 to Vertex 1 is 0
The distance of Vertex 1 to Vertex 2 is 1
The distance of Vertex 1 to Vertex 3 is 4

The distance of Vertex 2 to Vertex 1 is 2
The distance of Vertex 2 to Vertex 2 is 0
There is not direct edge between 2 and 3

The distance of Vertex 3 to Vertex 1 is 3
There is not direct edge between 3 and 2
The distance of Vertex 3 to Vertex 3 is 0

Matrix formed is
  0   1   4
  2   0   Inf
  3   Inf   0
--------------------------------------------------------------------------


Shortest Path between the vertices

Shortest Path from Vertex 1 to Vertex 1 is 0
Shortest Path from Vertex 1 to Vertex 2 is 1
Shortest Path from Vertex 1 to Vertex 3 is 4
Shortest Path from Vertex 2 to Vertex 1 is 2
Shortest Path from Vertex 2 to Vertex 2 is 0
Shortest Path from Vertex 2 to Vertex 3 is 6
Shortest Path from Vertex 3 to Vertex 1 is 3
Shortest Path from Vertex 3 to Vertex 2 is 4
Shortest Path from Vertex 3 to Vertex 3 is 0

Shortest path Matrix formed is
  0   1   4
  2   0   6
  3   4   0
--------------------------------------------------------------------------
```

```
    For Bus topology
Initial State of the graph

The distance of Vertex 1 to Vertex 1 is 0
The distance of Vertex 1 to Vertex 2 is 1
The distance of Vertex 1 to Vertex 3 is 2

The distance of Vertex 2 to Vertex 1 is 1
The distance of Vertex 2 to Vertex 2 is 0
The distance of Vertex 2 to Vertex 3 is 1

The distance of Vertex 3 to Vertex 1 is 2
The distance of Vertex 3 to Vertex 2 is 1
The distance of Vertex 3 to Vertex 3 is 0

Matrix formed is
  0   1   2
  1   0   1
  2   1   0
-----------------------------------------------------------------------


Shortest Path between the vertices

Shortest Path from Vertex 1 to Vertex 1 is 0
Shortest Path from Vertex 1 to Vertex 2 is 1
Shortest Path from Vertex 1 to Vertex 3 is 2
Shortest Path from Vertex 2 to Vertex 1 is 1
Shortest Path from Vertex 2 to Vertex 2 is 0
Shortest Path from Vertex 2 to Vertex 3 is 1
Shortest Path from Vertex 3 to Vertex 1 is 2
Shortest Path from Vertex 3 to Vertex 2 is 1
Shortest Path from Vertex 3 to Vertex 3 is 0

Shortest path Matrix formed is
  0   1   2
  1   0   1
  2   1   0
-----------------------------------------------------------------------
```

2.29   NtgLocality and NtgLocalityConnex

```
n=100;//network size
l=1000;//network squared area side
d=100;//Locality radius
[g]=NtgLocalityConnex(n,l,d);//application of NtgLocalityConnex
[g1]=NtgLocality(n,l,d);//application of NtgLocality
show_graph(g1);
show_graph(g);
```

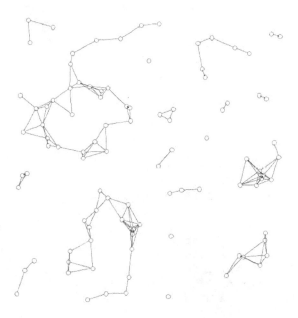

Figure 2.15: NtgLocality and NtgLocalityConnex

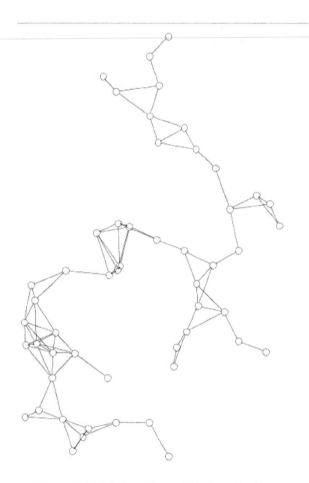

Figure 2.16: NtgLocality and NtgLocalityConnex

2.30 Network topology generation Waxmann Comparison

```
a=0.1;//first parameter of the Waxman model
b=0.8;//second parameter of the Waxman model
n=100;//network size
l=1000;//network squared area side
//application of NtgWaxmanConnex
[g]=NtgWaxmanConnex(a,b,n,l);
show_graph(g);
//NTGWaxMan
[g1,d]=NtgWaxman(a,b,n,l);//application of NtgWaxman
show_graph(g1);
scf(1);clf(1);
plot(d);
plot2d3(d);
xtitle('','node index','degree');
```

h

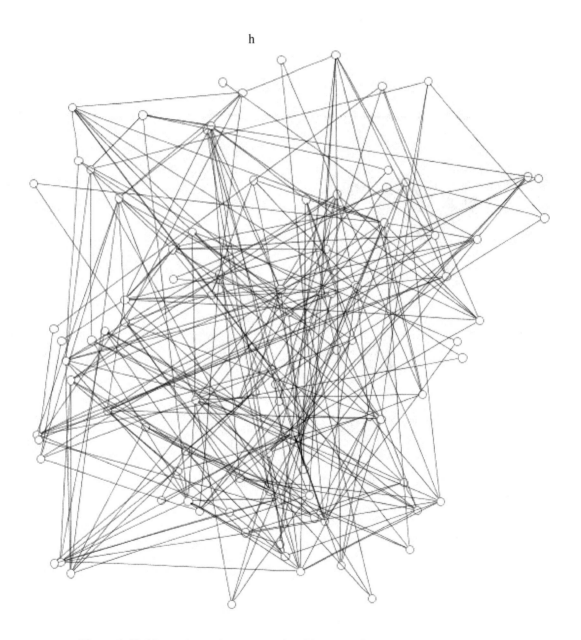

Figure 2.17: Network topology generation Waxmann Comparison

h

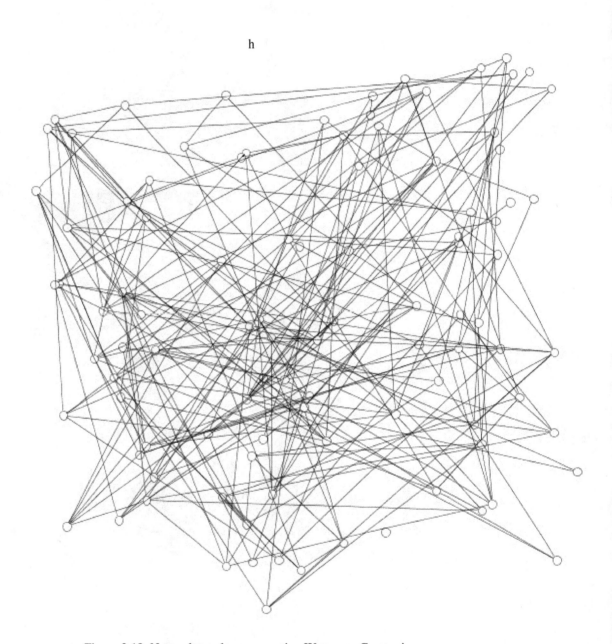

Figure 2.18: Network topology generation Waxmann Comparison

h

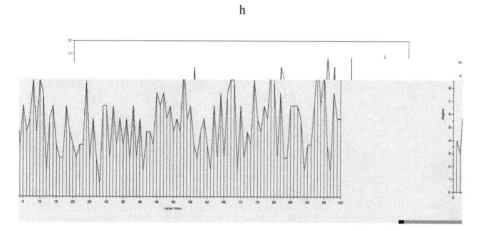

Figure 2.19: Network topology generation Waxmann Comparison

2.31   Routing Table optimization using Dijkstra

```
n=80;//network size
l=1000;//network squared area side
d=100;//Locality radius
[g]=NtgLocalityConnex(n,l,d);//generation of a topology
show_graph(g);
[rt2]=RoutingTableDijkstra(g);//application of
    RoutingTableDijkstra
///using shortest rounting table (Routing Shortest Rt)
rt=[rt2 zeros(l,2)];//addition of two empty columns
rt(1:10,:)//initial state
[rt]=RoutingShortestRT(rt);//application of RoutingShortestRT
rt(1:10,:)//final state
rt
```

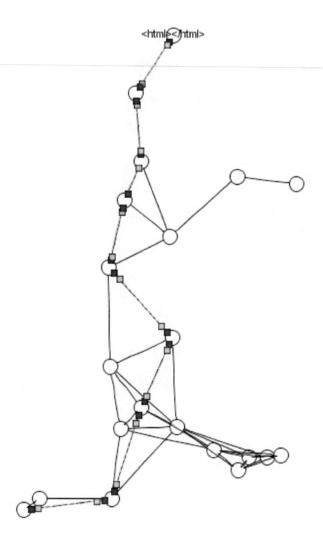

Figure 2.20: Routing Table optimization using Dijkstra

2.32   RoutingTable Flood and Bellmanford

```
n=80;//network size
l=1000;//network squared area side
d=100;//Locality radius
[g]=NtgLocalityConnex(n,l,d);//generation of a topology
show_graph(g);
TTL=10;//Flood Time-To-Live
[rt]=RoutingTableFlood(g,TTL);//application of
    RoutingTableFlood
i=Random(length(g.node_x));//selection of the source node
EB=ones(1,length(g.node_x));//display the source node
EC=ones(1,length(g.node_x));
EB(i)=3;
EC(i)=5;
g.node_border=EB;
g.node_color=EC;
show_graph(g);
[dist,pred]=RoutingBellmanFord(g,i);//Application of
    RoutingBellmanFord
```

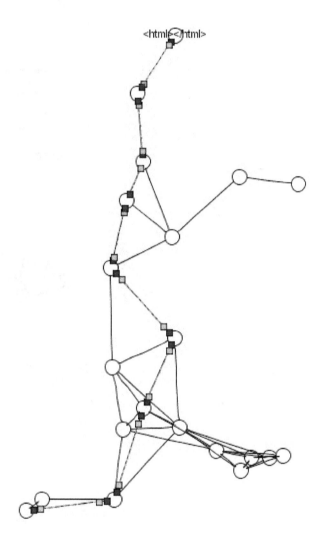

Figure 2.21: RoutingTable Flood and Bellmanford

2.33 Routing using BFS and DFS

```
n=150;//network size
L=1000;//network square area side
dmax=100;//Locality radius
[g]=NtgLocalityConnex(n,L,dmax);//generation of a topology in
    respect with the Locality method
i=Random(length(g.node_x));//selection of the source node
dw=6;//display parameter
[v,pred]=RoutingBFSWeight(g,i,dw);//application of
    RoutingBFSWeight
//DEPTH FIRST SEARCH
i=Random(length(g.node_x));//selection of the source node
dw=2;//display parameter
[v,pred]=RoutingDFS(g,i,dw);//application of RoutingDFS
```

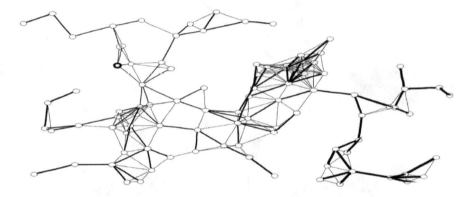

Figure 2.22: Routing using BFS and DFS

h!

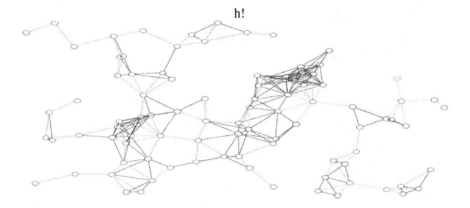

Figure 2.23: Routing using BFS and DFS

2.34　Weight graph generation

```
n=90;      //network size
L=500;        //network square area side
dmax=100;       //locality radius
[g]=NtgLocalityConnex(n,L,dmax);    //generation of a random
    topology in respect with the Locality method.
show_graph(g);
g.edges.data.length=[]
[g]=EdgeLength(g);        //application of EdgeLength
g.edges.data.length
```

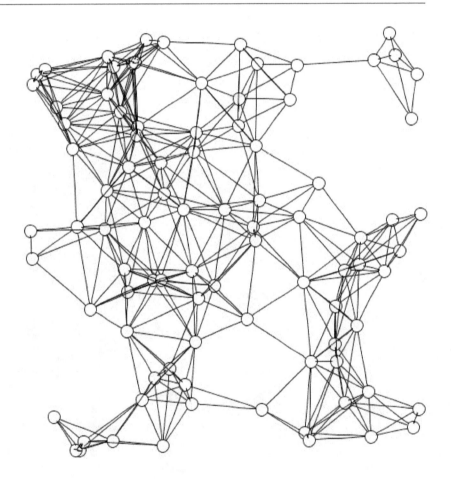

2.35   Shortest path between two nodes using Dijkstra

```
clc ; // clear command window
clear ; // This command kills variables which are not protected
            .
funcprot(0) // Scilab functions are variable, funcprot allows
      the user to specify what scilab do when such variables are
      redefined.
function[l]=short(adj,weight,inc,colincrease,n) // creating
      fuction and defining variables
for row =1:n // applying for loop from source
 for col =1:n // applying loop for checking other nodes(loop2)
  if(weight((row-1)*n+col)==0) // checking for adjacent node
   weight((row-1)*n+col)=9999; // weight infinity to those which
        are not connected to selected node
  end
 end
end
distance=[]; // creating array distance
perm=[]; // creating array perm
for row =1:n // calulate distance between nodes
 distance=[distance(:,:),9999]; // Stores the distance between
      nodes
 perm =[perm(:,:),0]; // check for the minimum distance
end
perm(inc)=1; // set source = 1 you can change it also
distance(inc)=0; // set intial distance = 0
current =inc;
while(current ~= colincrease) // move your loop2 for changing
      values
smalldist =9999; // create an variable used for changing
      distance
dc= distance(current); // dc will store change distance used in
      cslculating new distance
for row =1:n
 if( perm(row)==0)
  newdist =dc+weight((current -1)*n+row); // calculate the new
      distnace
  if( newdist < distance(row)) // comparing and changing the
      distance to minimum distance using this condition
   distance(row)= newdist ;
  end
  if(distance(row)<smalldist) // comparinng all available paths
        using this condition
   smalldist = distance(row);
   krow=row;
  end
 end
end
```

```
current =krow;
perm (current)=1;
end
l=distance(colincrease);
printf ("The s h o r t e s t path between %d and %d i s %d" ,
    inc,colincrease,l); // print distance between souce and
    destination
endfunction

// It is values we have taken as example suppose here we are
    taking source as 1 and destination as n=3 we can change
    values according to our need
n =3;
adj =[0 1 1 0 0 1 0 0 0] // vertices connected to the adjacent
    nodess
weight =[0 12 22 0 0 9 0 0 0] // weight of the edges
short(adj,weight,1,3,n);
```

Result

The s h o r t e s t path between 1 and 3 i s 21

2.36   Floydwarshall algorithm Creation

```
//Implementation of floyd warshall routing algorithm for
   differnt topologies



clc ;
clear ;
funcprot (0)
function [ path ]= flyodwarshall(mat ,nodes)//calling the
   floydwarshall function


  //printing Initial state of the graph using matrix
  printf("\nInitial State of the graph\n");//printing simple
     string message
  for vertexi=1: nodes//starting for loop
     for vertexj=1: nodes//starting for loop
        if(mat((vertexi -1)*nodes+vertexj)==%inf)//if
           condition for checking content of matrix as inf
          printf("\nThere is not direct edge between %d and %
             d",vertexi,vertexj);//printing vertices not
             having direct edgees
          else//else condition
        printf("\nThe distance of Vertex %d to Vertex %d is %d
           ",vertexi,vertexj,mat ((vertexi -1)*nodes+vertexj)
           );//printing edge length between two vertices
        end//ending if condition
     end//ending for loop
     printf("\n");//printing new line
  end//ending for loop

  //printing Initial matrix
  printf("\nMatrix formed is\n");//printing simple string
     message
  for vertexi=1: nodes//starting for loop for row
     for vertexj=1: nodes//staring for loop for column
        printf(" %d ",mat ((vertexi -1)*nodes+vertexj));//
           printing i th and j th element of matrix
     end//ending inner for loop1
     printf("\n");//printing new line
  end//ending for loop



  //floyd warshall algorithm
  for vertexi =1: nodes//starting for loop for row
     for vertexj =1: nodes//staring for loop for column
```

```
    path ((vertexi -1)*nodes+vertexj)=mat((vertexi -1) *nodes+
        vertexj);//calling path function
    end//ending inner for loop
end//ending for loop

for vertexk =1: nodes//staring for loop
    for vertexi =1: nodes//staring for loop
            for vertexj =1: nodes//starting for loop
            if( (path ((vertexi -1) *nodes+vertexk) + path((
                vertexk -1)*nodes+vertexj)) < path((vertexi
                -1)*nodes+vertexj))//if condition
                path((vertexi -1)*nodes+vertexj)=path ((
                    vertexi -1) *nodes+vertexk) + path((
                    vertexk -1)*nodes+vertexj);//calling path
                    function
            end//ending if condition
        end//ending for loop
    end//ending for loop
end//ending for loop

//printing shortest path between two vertices
printf("
    ----------------        ------------------------------------------
    ");//simple print statement for printing string
printf ("\n\nShortest Path between the vertices\n\n");//
    simple print statemnet for printing string

for vertexi =1: nodes//starting for loop
    for vertexj =1: nodes//starting for loop
        printf ("Shortest Path from Vertex %d to Vertex %d is %d\
            n" ,vertexi,vertexj, path ((vertexi -1)*nodes+vertexj
            ));//printing shortest path from vertex i to vertex j
    end//ending for loop
end//ending for loop
//printing shortest path matrix
printf("\nShortest path Matrix formed is\n");//printing
    simple string message
for vertexi=1: nodes//staring for loop
    for vertexj=1: nodes//staring for loop
        printf(" %d ",path ((vertexi -1)*nodes+vertexj));//
            printing i th and j th element of matrix
    end//ending for loop
    printf("\n");//printing new line
    end//ending for loop

endfunction//ending function
printf("For Tree topology");//printing simple string message

nodes=3;
mat=[0 1 4 2 0 %inf 3 %inf 0]
```

```
path=flyodwarshall(mat ,nodes)

printf("For Bus topology");

n=3;
mat=[0 1 2 1 0 1 2 1 0]
path=flyodwarshall(mat ,nodes)
```

Result

```
 For Tree topology
Initial State of the graph

The distance of Vertex 1 to Vertex 1 is 0
The distance of Vertex 1 to Vertex 2 is 1
The distance of Vertex 1 to Vertex 3 is 4

The distance of Vertex 2 to Vertex 1 is 2
The distance of Vertex 2 to Vertex 2 is 0
There is not direct edge between 2 and 3

The distance of Vertex 3 to Vertex 1 is 3
There is not direct edge between 3 and 2
The distance of Vertex 3 to Vertex 3 is 0

Matrix formed is
  0    1    4
  2    0    Inf
  3    Inf  0
-------------------------------------------------------------------


Shortest Path between the vertices

Shortest Path from Vertex 1 to Vertex 1 is 0
Shortest Path from Vertex 1 to Vertex 2 is 1
Shortest Path from Vertex 1 to Vertex 3 is 4
Shortest Path from Vertex 2 to Vertex 1 is 2
Shortest Path from Vertex 2 to Vertex 2 is 0
Shortest Path from Vertex 2 to Vertex 3 is 6
Shortest Path from Vertex 3 to Vertex 1 is 3
Shortest Path from Vertex 3 to Vertex 2 is 4
Shortest Path from Vertex 3 to Vertex 3 is 0

Shortest path Matrix formed is
  0    1    4
  2    0    6
  3    4    0
For Bus topology
Initial State of the graph
```

```
The distance of Vertex 1 to Vertex 1 is 0
The distance of Vertex 1 to Vertex 2 is 1
The distance of Vertex 1 to Vertex 3 is 2

The distance of Vertex 2 to Vertex 1 is 1
The distance of Vertex 2 to Vertex 2 is 0
The distance of Vertex 2 to Vertex 3 is 1

The distance of Vertex 3 to Vertex 1 is 2
The distance of Vertex 3 to Vertex 2 is 1
The distance of Vertex 3 to Vertex 3 is 0

Matrix formed is
  0   1   2
  1   0   1
  2   1   0
---------------------------------------------------------------------


Shortest Path between the vertices

Shortest Path from Vertex 1 to Vertex 1 is 0
Shortest Path from Vertex 1 to Vertex 2 is 1
Shortest Path from Vertex 1 to Vertex 3 is 2
Shortest Path from Vertex 2 to Vertex 1 is 1
Shortest Path from Vertex 2 to Vertex 2 is 0
Shortest Path from Vertex 2 to Vertex 3 is 1
Shortest Path from Vertex 3 to Vertex 1 is 2
Shortest Path from Vertex 3 to Vertex 2 is 1
Shortest Path from Vertex 3 to Vertex 3 is 0

Shortest path Matrix formed is
  0   1   2
  1   0   1
  2   1   0
```

2.37   BellmanFord Comparison

```
//School of Computing Science and Engineering
//VIT Chennai

//Code to compute the CPU time taken by the BellmanFord routing
    algorithm to return the
//Vector of the total distance between each network node and
    the source node and
//Vector composed by the predecessor of each node in order to
    reach the source
//node in respect with the shortest path for various network
    sizes.

//Clear display and environment variables
clc
clear all

//Creating a random topology which is tiny in size
network_size=80;            //network size is 80
net_square_area=1000;            //network square area side is
    1000
locality_radius=100;            //locality radius is 100
[g]=NL_T_LocalityConnex(network_size,net_square_area,
    locality_radius); //generation of a random topology in
    respect with the Locality method.
iteration=NL_F_RandInt1n(length(g.node_x)); //selection of the
    source node
window_index=1;            //window index
g.node_diam(iteration)=40; //node diameter
g.node_border(iteration)=10; //node border
g.node_color(iteration)=5; //node color
[f]=NL_G_ShowGraphN(g,window_index);//graph visualization
//Application of the BellmanFord algorithm
for iteration = 1:30            //Run 30 iterations
   timer();            //Initialize timer
   [dist,pred]=NL_R_BellmanFord(g,iteration); //application of
      NL_R_BellmanFord
   A(iteration) = timer()      //Store timer value in array
end
average_time=mean(A);            //Calculate average time taken
disp(average_time,"Tiny:")      //Display average time


//Creating a random topology which is small in size
network_size=90;            //network size is 90
[g]=NL_T_LocalityConnex(network_size,net_square_area,
    locality_radius); //generation of a random topology in
```

```
    respect with the Locality method.
iteration=NL_F_RandInt1n(length(g.node_x)); //selection of the
    source node
g.node_diam(iteration)=40; //node diameter
g.node_border(iteration)=10; //node border
g.node_color(iteration)=5;
window_index=2;      //node color
[f]=NL_G_ShowGraphN(g,window_index);//graph visualization
//Application of the BellmanFord algorithm
for iteration = 1:30          //Run 30 iterations
    timer();            //Initialize timer
    [dist,pred]=NL_R_BellmanFord(g,iteration); //application of
        NL_R_BellmanFord
    A(iteration) = timer()      //Store timer value in array
end
average_time=mean(A);          //Calculate average time taken
disp(average_time,"Small:")    //Display average time


//Creating a random topology which is medium in size
network_size=120;          //network size is 120
[g]=NL_T_LocalityConnex(network_size,net_square_area,
    locality_radius); //generation of a random topology in
    respect with the Locality method.
iteration=NL_F_RandInt1n(length(g.node_x)); //selection of the
    source node
g.node_diam(iteration)=40; //node diameter
g.node_border(iteration)=10; //node border
g.node_color(iteration)=5; //node color
window_index=3;
[f]=NL_G_ShowGraphN(g,window_index);//graph visualization
//Application of the BellmanFord algorithm
for iteration = 1:30          //Run 30 iterations
    timer();            //Initialize timer
    [dist,pred]=NL_R_BellmanFord(g,iteration); //application of
        NL_R_BellmanFord
    A(iteration) = timer()      //Store timer value in array
end
average_time=mean(A);          //Calculate average time taken
disp(average_time,"Medium:")    //Display average time


//Creating a random topology which is large in size
network_size=150;          //network size is 150
[g]=NL_T_LocalityConnex(network_size,net_square_area,
    locality_radius); //generation of a random topology in
    respect with the Locality method.
iteration=NL_F_RandInt1n(length(g.node_x)); //selection of the
    source node
g.node_diam(iteration)=40; //node diameter
```

```
g.node_border(iteration)=10;  //node border
g.node_color(iteration)=5;  //node color
window_index=4;
[f]=NL_G_ShowGraphN(g,window_index);//graph visualization
//Application of the BellmanFord algorithm
for iteration = 1:30          //Run 30 iterations
   timer();              //Initialize timer
   [dist,pred]=NL_R_BellmanFord(g,iteration); //application of
      NL_R_BellmanFord
   A(iteration) = timer()      //Store timer value in array
end
average_time=mean(A);           //Calculate average time taken
disp(average_time,"Large:")     //Display average time


//Creating a random topology which is very large in size
network_size=180;              //network size is 180
[g]=NL_T_LocalityConnex(network_size,net_square_area,
   locality_radius); //generation of a random topology in
   respect with the Locality method.
iteration=NL_F_RandInt1n(length(g.node_x)); //selection of the
   source node
g.node_diam(iteration)=40; //node diameter
g.node_border(iteration)=10; //node border
g.node_color(iteration)=5; //node color
window_index=5;
[f]=NL_G_ShowGraphN(g,window_index);//graph visualization
//Application of the BellmanFord algorithm
for iteration = 1:30          //Run 30 iterations
   timer();              //Initialize timer
   [dist,pred]=NL_R_BellmanFord(g,iteration); //application of
      NL_R_BellmanFord
   A(iteration) = timer()      //Store timer value in array
end
average_time=mean(A);           //Calculate average time taken
disp(average_time,"Very Large:")    //Display average time
```

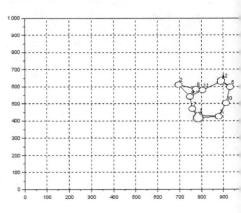

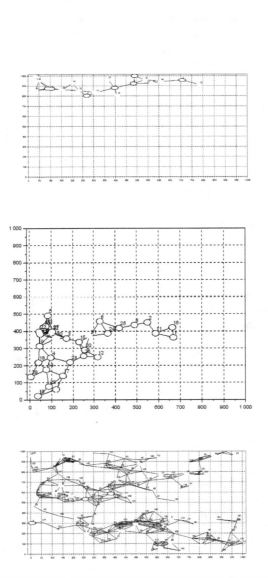

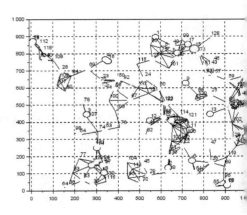

```
Tiny      : 0.0177083
Small     : 0.0140625
Medium    : 0.1192708
Large     : 0.2213542
Very Large : 1.0411458
```

2.38 BellmanFord Comparison Plot

```
//School of Computing Science and Engineering
//VIT Chennai

//Code to compute the CPU time taken by the BellmanFord routing
    algorithm to return the
//Vector of the total distance between each network node and
   the source node and
//Vector composed by the predecessor of each node in order to
   reach the source
//node in respect with the shortest path for various network
   sizes.

//Clear display and environment variables

clc;
clear all;

//Creating a random topology which is tiny in size
   variable3 = 1;
   variable2 = 1;
for nodes=10:10:160
   b(variable3) = nodes;
   net_square_area=1000;              //network square area size is
       1000
   locality_radius=100;              //locality radius is 100

//   networkname = "Routing using BellmanFord Algorithm";
   [g]=NL_T_LocalityConnex(nodes,net_square_area,
       locality_radius); //generation of a random topology in
       respect with the Locality method.

   variable1=NL_F_RandInt1n(length(g.node_x)); //selection of
       the source node
   window_index=1;                   //window index
   g.node_diam(variable1)=40; //node diameter
   g.node_border(variable1)=10; //node border
   g.node_color(variable1)=5; //node color
   [f]=NL_G_ShowGraphN(g,window_index);//graph visualization

//Application of the BellmanFord algorithm
   for variable1 = 1:5              //Run 5 iterations
       timer();                 //Initialize timer
       [dist,pred]=NL_R_BellmanFord(g,variable1); //application
           of NL_R_BellmanFord
       A(variable1) = timer()     //Store timer value in array
   end
```

```
        average_time(variable2)=mean(A);          //Calculate average
            time taken
        disp(average_time(variable2),nodes,"Time of finding the
            shortest path for nodes",) //Display average time
        variable2 = variable2+1;
        variable3 = variable3+1;
end
clf();
for x = average_time
    for y = b
        disp('Time of Computation for BellmanFord Algorithm')
        disp('Nodes')
        disp(y);
        disp('Time for Execution (Respectively)');
        disp(x);
        plot(b,average_time,'--mo');
        xtitle( 'Time of Computation for BellmanFord Algorithm',
            'Number of Nodes', 'Time', boxed = %t );
    end
end
```

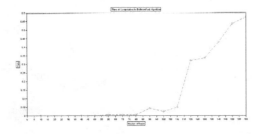

```
Time of Computation for BellmanFord Algorithm

Nodes

    10.
    20.
    30.
    40.
    50.
    60.
    70.
    80.
    90.
    100.
    110.
    120.
    130.
    140.
```

```
150.
160.
```

Time for Execution (Respectively)

```
0.
0.
0.
0.
0.
0.00625
0.00625
0.00625
0.04375
0.025
0.05
0.321875
0.3375
0.43125
0.5375
0.575
```

2.39   BFS Comparison

```
//School of Computing Science and Engineering
//VIT Chennai

//Code to compute the CPU time taken by the BFS routing
    algorithm to return the
//Vector of the total distance between each network node and
    the source node and
//Vector composed by the predecessor of each node in order to
    reach the source
//node in respect with the shortest path for various network
    sizes.

//Clear display and environment variables
clc
clear all

//Creating a random topology which is tiny in size
network_size=80;              //network size is 80
net_square_area=1000;               //network square area side is
    1000
locality_radius=100;          //locality radius is 100
[g]=NL_T_LocalityConnex(network_size,net_square_area,
    locality_radius); //generation of a random topology in
    respect with the Locality method.
iteration=NL_F_RandInt1n(length(g.node_x)); //selection of the
    source node
window_index=1;               //window index
g.node_diam(iteration)=40; //node diameter
g.node_border(iteration)=10; //node border
g.node_color(iteration)=5; //node color
[f]=NL_G_ShowGraphN(g,window_index);//graph visualization

//Application of the BFS algorithm
for iteration = 1:30          //Run 30 iterations
    timer();          //Initialize timer
    [dist,pred]=NL_R_BFS(g,iteration); //application of NL_R_BFS
    A(iteration) = timer()     //Store timer value in array
end
average_time=mean(A);               //Calculate average time taken
disp(average_time,"Tiny:")     //Display average time


//Creating a random topology which is small in size
network_size=90;              //network size is 90
[g]=NL_T_LocalityConnex(network_size,net_square_area,
    locality_radius); //generation of a random topology in
```

```
   respect with the Locality method.
iteration=NL_F_RandInt1n(length(g.node_x)); //selection of the
   source node
g.node_diam(iteration)=40; //node diameter
g.node_border(iteration)=10; //node border
g.node_color(iteration)=5;
window_index=2;    //node color
[f]=NL_G_ShowGraphN(g,window_index);//graph visualization
//Application of the BFS algorithm
for iteration = 1:30          //Run 30 iterations
   timer();              //Initialize timer
   [dist,pred]=NL_R_BFS(g,iteration); //application of NL_R_BFS
   A(iteration) = timer()    //Store timer value in array
end
average_time=mean(A);         //Calculate average time taken
disp(average_time,"Small:")      //Display average time


//Creating a random topology which is medium in size
network_size=120;             //network size is 120
[g]=NL_T_LocalityConnex(network_size,net_square_area,
   locality_radius); //generation of a random topology in
   respect with the Locality method.
iteration=NL_F_RandInt1n(length(g.node_x)); //selection of the
   source node
g.node_diam(iteration)=40; //node diameter
g.node_border(iteration)=10; //node border
g.node_color(iteration)=5; //node color
window_index=3;
[f]=NL_G_ShowGraphN(g,window_index);//graph visualization
//Application of the BFS algorithm
for iteration = 1:30          //Run 30 iterations
   timer();              //Initialize timer
   [dist,pred]=NL_R_BFS(g,iteration); //application of NL_R_BFS
   A(iteration) = timer()    //Store timer value in array
end
average_time=mean(A);         //Calculate average time taken
disp(average_time,"Medium:")      //Display average time


//Creating a random topology which is large in size
network_size=150;             //network size is 150
[g]=NL_T_LocalityConnex(network_size,net_square_area,
   locality_radius); //generation of a random topology in
   respect with the Locality method.
iteration=NL_F_RandInt1n(length(g.node_x)); //selection of the
   source node
g.node_diam(iteration)=40; //node diameter
g.node_border(iteration)=10; //node border
g.node_color(iteration)=5; //node color
```

```
window_index=4;
[f]=NL_G_ShowGraphN(g,window_index);//graph visualization
//Application of the BFS algorithm
for iteration = 1:30            //Run 30 iterations
    timer();                    //Initialize timer
    [dist,pred]=NL_R_BFS(g,iteration); //application of NL_R_BFS
    A(iteration) = timer()      //Store timer value in array
end
average_time=mean(A);                //Calculate average time taken
disp(average_time,"Large:")          //Display average time


//Creating a random topology which is very large in size
network_size=180;               //network size is 180
[g]=NL_T_LocalityConnex(network_size,net_square_area,
    locality_radius); //generation of a random topology in
    respect with the Locality method.
iteration=NL_F_RandInt1n(length(g.node_x)); //selection of the
        source node
g.node_diam(iteration)=40; //node diameter
g.node_border(iteration)=10; //node border
g.node_color(iteration)=5; //node color
window_index=5;
[f]=NL_G_ShowGraphN(g,window_index);//graph visualization
//Application of the BFS algorithm
for iteration = 1:30            //Run 30 iterations
    timer();                    //Initialize timer
    [dist,pred]=NL_R_BFS(g,iteration); //application of NL_R_BFS
    A(iteration) = timer()      //Store timer value in array
end
average_time=mean(A);                //Calculate average time taken
disp(average_time,"Very Large:")      //Display average time
```

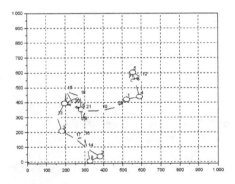 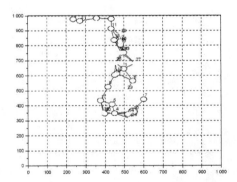

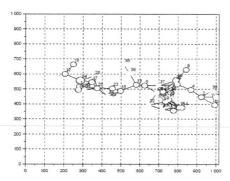

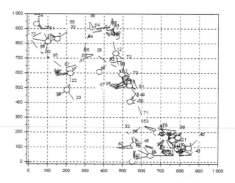

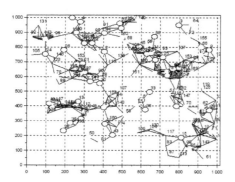

Tiny	:	0.0114583
Small	:	0.015625
Medium	:	0.0244792
Large	:	0.0494792
Very Large	:	0.0890625

2.40   BFS Comparison Plot

```
//Authors:

//School of Computing Science and Engineering
//VIT Chennai

//Code to compute the CPU time taken by the BFS routing
    algorithm to return the
//Vector of the total distance between each network node and
    the source node and
//Vector composed by the predecessor of each node in order to
    reach the source
//node in respect with the shortest path for various network
    sizes.

//Clear display and environment variables

clc;
clear all;

//Creating a random topology which is tiny in size
    variable3 = 1;
    variable2 = 1;
for nodes=10:10:160
    b(variable3) = nodes;
    net_square_area=1000;             //network square area size is
        1000
    locality_radius=100;             //locality radius is 100

//   networkname = "Routing using BFS Algorithm";
    [g]=NL_T_LocalityConnex(nodes,net_square_area,
        locality_radius); //generation of a random topology in
        respect with the Locality method.

    variable1=NL_F_RandInt1n(length(g.node_x)); //selection of
        the source node
    window_index=1;                 //window index
    g.node_diam(variable1)=40; //node diameter
    g.node_border(variable1)=10; //node border
    g.node_color(variable1)=5; //node color
    [f]=NL_G_ShowGraphN(g,window_index);//graph visualization

//Application of the BFS algorithm
    for variable1 = 1:5              //Run 5 iterations
        timer();               //Initialize timer
        [dist,pred]=NL_R_BFS(g,variable1); //application of
            NL_R_BFS
        A(variable1) = timer()      //Store timer value in array
```

```
      end
      average_time(variable2)=mean(A);          //Calculate average
          time taken
      disp(average_time(variable2),nodes,"Time of finding the
          shortest path for nodes",) //Display average time
      variable2 = variable2+1;
      variable3 = variable3+1;
end
clf();
for x = average_time
    for y = b
        disp('Time of Computation for BFS Algorithm')
        disp('Nodes')
        disp(y);
        disp('Time for Execution (Respectively)');
        disp(x);
        plot(b,average_time,'--mo');
        xtitle( 'Time of Computation for BFS Algorithm', 'Number
            of Nodes', 'Time', boxed = %t );
    end
end
```

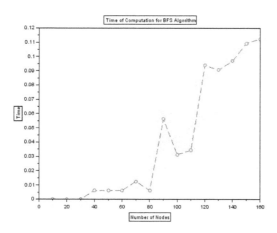

```
Time of Computation for BFS Algorithm
Nodes

    10.
    20.
    30.
    40.
    50.
    60.
    70.
    80.
```

```
90.
100.
110.
120.
130.
140.
150.
160.
```

Time for Execution (Respectively)

```
0.
0.
0.
0.00625
0.00625
0.00625
0.0125
0.00625
0.05625
0.03125
0.034375
0.09375
0.090625
0.096875
0.109375
0.1125
```

2.41 BFS Weight Comparison

```
//Authors:

//School of Computing Science and Engineering
//VIT Chennai

//Code to compute the CPU time taken by the BFSWeight routing
    algorithm to return the
//Vector of the total distance between each network node and
    the source node and
//Vector composed by the predecessor of each node in order to
    reach the source
//node in respect with the shortest path for various network
    sizes.

//Clear display and environment variables
clc
clear all

//Creating a random topology which is tiny in size
network_size=80;              //network size is 80
net_square_area=1000;            //network square area side is
    1000
locality_radius=100;          //locality radius is 100
[g]=NL_T_LocalityConnex(network_size,net_square_area,
    locality_radius); //generation of a random topology in
    respect with the Locality method.
iteration=NL_F_RandInt1n(length(g.node_x)); //selection of the
    source node
window_index=1;                //window index
g.node_diam(iteration)=40; //node diameter
g.node_border(iteration)=10; //node border
g.node_color(iteration)=5; //node color
[f]=NL_G_ShowGraphN(g,window_index);//graph visualization

//Application of the BFSWeight algorithm
for iteration = 1:30              //Run 30 iterations
   timer();             //Initialize timer
   [dist,pred]=NL_R_BFSWeight(g,iteration); //application of
      NL_R_BFSWeight
   A(iteration) = timer()      //Store timer value in array
end
average_time=mean(A);           //Calculate average time taken
disp(average_time,"Tiny:")      //Display average time


//Creating a random topology which is small in size
network_size=90;                //network size is 90
```

```
[g]=NL_T_LocalityConnex(network_size,net_square_area,
    locality_radius); //generation of a random topology in
    respect with the Locality method.
iteration=NL_F_RandInt1n(length(g.node_x)); //selection of the
    source node
g.node_diam(iteration)=40; //node diameter
g.node_border(iteration)=10; //node border
g.node_color(iteration)=5; //node color
window_index=2;
[f]=NL_G_ShowGraphN(g,window_index);//graph visualization
//Application of the BFSWeight algorithm
for iteration = 1:30           //Run 30 iterations
    timer();                   //Initialize timer
    [dist,pred]=NL_R_BFSWeight(g,iteration); //application of
        NL_R_BFSWeight
    A(iteration) = timer()     //Store timer value in array
end
average_time=mean(A);          //Calculate average time taken
disp(average_time,"Small:")    //Display average time


//Creating a random topology which is medium in size
network_size=120;
window_index=3;                //network size is 120
[g]=NL_T_LocalityConnex(network_size,net_square_area,
    locality_radius); //generation of a random topology in
    respect with the Locality method.
iteration=NL_F_RandInt1n(length(g.node_x)); //selection of the
    source node
g.node_diam(iteration)=40; //node diameter
g.node_border(iteration)=10; //node border
g.node_color(iteration)=5; //node color
[f]=NL_G_ShowGraphN(g,window_index);//graph visualization
//Application of the BFSWeight algorithm
for iteration = 1:30           //Run 30 iterations
    timer();                   //Initialize timer
    [dist,pred]=NL_R_BFSWeight(g,iteration); //application of
        NL_R_BFSWeight
    A(iteration) = timer()     //Store timer value in array
end
average_time=mean(A);          //Calculate average time taken
disp(average_time,"Medium:")   //Display average time


//Creating a random topology which is large in size
network_size=150;
window_index=4;                //network size is 150
[g]=NL_T_LocalityConnex(network_size,net_square_area,
    locality_radius); //generation of a random topology in
    respect with the Locality method.
```

```
iteration=NL_F_RandInt1n(length(g.node_x)); //selection of the
    source node
g.node_diam(iteration)=40; //node diameter
g.node_border(iteration)=10; //node border
g.node_color(iteration)=5; //node color
[f]=NL_G_ShowGraphN(g,window_index);//graph visualization
//Application of the BFSWeight algorithm
for iteration = 1:30          //Run 30 iterations
    timer();               //Initialize timer
    [dist,pred]=NL_R_BFSWeight(g,iteration); //application of
        NL_R_BFSWeight
    A(iteration) = timer()      //Store timer value in array
end
average_time=mean(A);             //Calculate average time taken
disp(average_time,"Large:")       //Display average time


//Creating a random topology which is very large in size
network_size=180;
window_index=5;                 //network size is 180
[g]=NL_T_LocalityConnex(network_size,net_square_area,
    locality_radius); //generation of a random topology in
    respect with the Locality method.
iteration=NL_F_RandInt1n(length(g.node_x)); //selection of the
    source node
g.node_diam(iteration)=40; //node diameter
g.node_border(iteration)=10; //node border
g.node_color(iteration)=5; //node color
[f]=NL_G_ShowGraphN(g,window_index);//graph visualization
//Application of the BFSWeight algorithm
for iteration = 1:30          //Run 30 iterations
    timer();               //Initialize timer
    [dist,pred]=NL_R_BFSWeight(g,iteration); //application of
        NL_R_BFSWeight
    A(iteration) = timer()      //Store timer value in array
end
average_time=mean(A);             //Calculate average time taken
disp(average_time,"Very Large:")    //Display average time
```

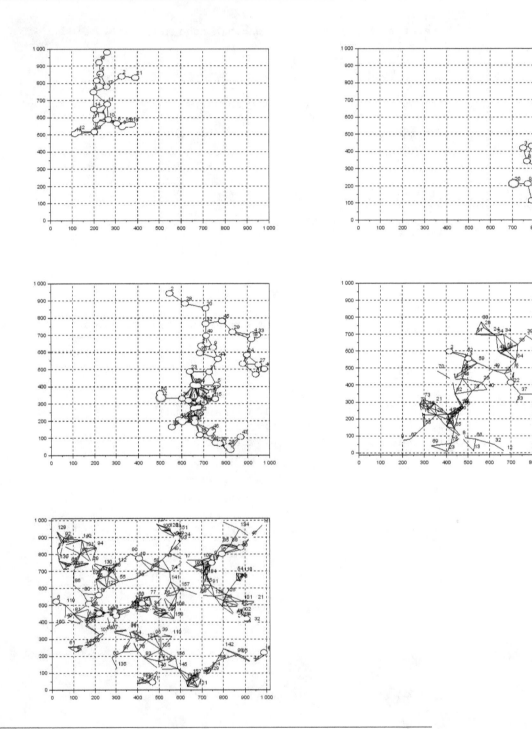

Tiny :   0.0104167

```
Small      :  0.009375
Medium     :  0.0416667
Large      :  0.034375
Very Large :  0.0765625
```

2.42   BFS Weight Comparison Plot

```
//Authors:

//School of Computing Science and Engineering
//VIT Chennai

//Code to compute the CPU time taken by the BFSWeight routing
    algorithm to return the
//Vector of the total distance between each network node and
    the source node and
//Vector composed by the predecessor of each node in order to
    reach the source
//node in respect with the shortest path for various network
    sizes.

//Clear display and environment variables

clc;
clear all;

//Creating a random topology which is tiny in size
    variable3 = 1;
    variable2 = 1;
for nodes=10:10:160
    b(variable3) = nodes;
    net_square_area=1000;              //network square area size is
        1000
    locality_radius=100;             //locality radius is 100

//   networkname = "Routing using BFSWeight Algorithm";
    [g]=NL_T_LocalityConnex(nodes,net_square_area,
        locality_radius); //generation of a random topology in
        respect with the Locality method.

    variable1=NL_F_RandInt1n(length(g.node_x)); //selection of
        the source node
    window_index=1;                  //window index
    g.node_diam(variable1)=40; //node diameter
    g.node_border(variable1)=10; //node border
    g.node_color(variable1)=5; //node color
    [f]=NL_G_ShowGraphN(g,window_index);//graph visualization

//Application of the BFSWeight algorithm
    for variable1 = 1:5              //Run 5 iterations
        timer();                 //Initialize timer
        [dist,pred]=NL_R_BFSWeight(g,variable1); //application of
            NL_R_BFSWeight
        A(variable1) = timer()     //Store timer value in array
```

```
      end
      average_time(variable2)=mean(A);         //Calculate average
         time taken
      disp(average_time(variable2),nodes,"Time of finding the
         shortest path for nodes",) //Display average time
      variable2 = variable2+1;
      variable3 = variable3+1;
end
clf();
for x = average_time
   for y = b
      disp('Time of Computation for BFSWeight Algorithm')
      disp('Nodes')
      disp(y);
      disp('Time for Execution (Respectively)');
      disp(x);
      plot(b,average_time,'--mo');
      xtitle( 'Time of Computation for BFSWeight Algorithm', '
         Number of Nodes', 'Time', boxed = %t );
   end
end
```

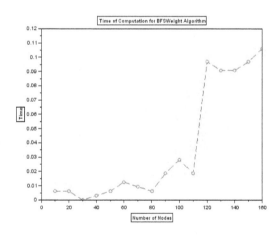

```
Time of Computation for BFSWeight Algorithm

Nodes

   10.
   20.
   30.
   40.
   50.
   60.
```

```
70.
80.
90.
100.
110.
120.
130.
140.
150.
160.

Time for Execution (Respectively)

0.00625
0.00625
0.
0.003125
0.00625
0.0125
0.009375
0.00625
0.01875
0.028125
0.01875
0.096875
0.090625
0.090625
0.096875
0.10625
```

2.43   DFS Comparison

```
//Authors:

//School of Computing Science and Engineering
//VIT Chennai

//Code to compute the CPU time taken by the DFS routing
    algorithm to return the
//Vector of the total distance between each network node and
    the source node and
//Vector composed by the predecessor of each node in order to
    reach the source
//node in respect with the shortest path for various network
    sizes.

//Clear display and environment variables
clc
clear all

//Creating a random topology which is tiny in size
network_size=80;            //network size is 80
net_square_area=1000;            //network square area side is
    1000
locality_radius=100;        //locality radius is 100
[g]=NL_T_LocalityConnex(network_size,net_square_area,
    locality_radius); //generation of a random topology in
    respect with the Locality method.
iteration=NL_F_RandInt1n(length(g.node_x)); //selection of the
    source node
ind=1;                //window index
g.node_diam(iteration)=40; //node diameter
g.node_border(iteration)=10; //node border
g.node_color(iteration)=5; //node color
[f]=NL_G_ShowGraphN(g,ind);//graph visualization
//Application of the DFS algorithm
for iteration = 1:30            //Run 30 iterations
    timer();            //Initialize timer
    [dist,pred]=NL_R_DFS(g,iteration); //application of NL_R_DFS
    A(iteration) = timer()        //Store timer value in array
end
average_time=mean(A);            //Calculate average time taken
disp(average_time,"Tiny:")        //Display average time


//Creating a random topology which is small in size
network_size=90;            //network size is 90
[g]=NL_T_LocalityConnex(network_size,net_square_area,
    locality_radius); //generation of a random topology in
```

```
    respect with the Locality method.
iteration=NL_F_RandInt1n(length(g.node_x)); //selection of the
    source node
g.node_diam(iteration)=40; //node diameter
g.node_border(iteration)=10; //node border
g.node_color(iteration)=5; //node color
ind=2;
[f]=NL_G_ShowGraphN(g,ind);//graph visualization
//Application of the DFS algorithm
for iteration = 1:30            //Run 30 iterations
    timer();              //Initialize timer
    [dist,pred]=NL_R_DFS(g,iteration); //application of NL_R_DFS
    A(iteration) = timer()      //Store timer value in array
end
average_time=mean(A);           //Calculate average time taken
disp(average_time,"Small:")     //Display average time


//Creating a random topology which is medium in size
network_size=120;               //network size is 120
[g]=NL_T_LocalityConnex(network_size,net_square_area,
    locality_radius); //generation of a random topology in
    respect with the Locality method.
iteration=NL_F_RandInt1n(length(g.node_x)); //selection of the
    source node
g.node_diam(iteration)=40; //node diameter
g.node_border(iteration)=10; //node border
g.node_color(iteration)=5; //node color
ind=3;
[f]=NL_G_ShowGraphN(g,ind);//graph visualization
//Application of the DFS algorithm
for iteration = 1:30            //Run 30 iterations
    timer();              //Initialize timer
    [dist,pred]=NL_R_DFS(g,iteration); //application of NL_R_DFS
    A(iteration) = timer()      //Store timer value in array
end
average_time=mean(A);           //Calculate average time taken
disp(average_time,"Medium:")    //Display average time


//Creating a random topology which is large in size
network_size=150;               //network size is 150
[g]=NL_T_LocalityConnex(network_size,net_square_area,
    locality_radius); //generation of a random topology in
    respect with the Locality method.
iteration=NL_F_RandInt1n(length(g.node_x)); //selection of the
    source node
g.node_diam(iteration)=40; //node diameter
g.node_border(iteration)=10; //node border
g.node_color(iteration)=5; //node color
```

```
ind=4;
[f]=NL_G_ShowGraphN(g,ind);//graph visualization
//Application of the DFS algorithm
for iteration = 1:30          //Run 30 iterations
    timer();                  //Initialize timer
    [dist,pred]=NL_R_DFS(g,iteration); //application of NL_R_DFS
    A(iteration) = timer()    //Store timer value in array
end
average_time=mean(A);         //Calculate average time taken
disp(average_time,"Large:")   //Display average time


//Creating a random topology which is very large in size
network_size=180;
ind=5;              //network size is 180
[g]=NL_T_LocalityConnex(network_size,net_square_area,
    locality_radius); //generation of a random topology in
    respect with the Locality method.
iteration=NL_F_RandInt1n(length(g.node_x)); //selection of the
    source node
g.node_diam(iteration)=40; //node diameter
g.node_border(iteration)=10; //node border
g.node_color(iteration)=5; //node color
[f]=NL_G_ShowGraphN(g,ind);//graph visualization
//Application of the DFS algorithm
for iteration = 1:30          //Run 30 iterations
    timer();                  //Initialize timer
    [dist,pred]=NL_R_DFS(g,iteration); //application of NL_R_DFS
    A(iteration) = timer()    //Store timer value in array
end
average_time=mean(A);         //Calculate average time taken
disp(average_time,"Very Large:")    //Display average time
```

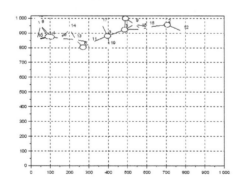
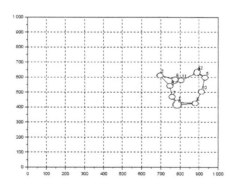

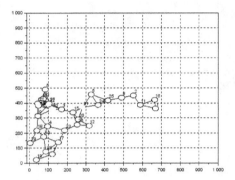
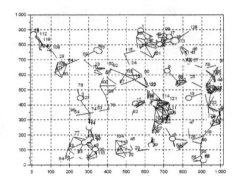
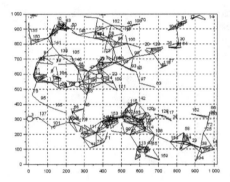

```
Tiny       :    0.009375
Small      :    0.0041667
Medium     :    0.0223958
Large      :    0.08125
Very Large :    0.0869792
```

2.44 BFS Comparison Plot

```
//Authors:

//School of Computing Science and Engineering
//VIT Chennai

//Code to compute the CPU time taken by the DFS routing
    algorithm to return the
//Vector of the total distance between each network node and
    the source node and
//Vector composed by the predecessor of each node in order to
    reach the source
//node in respect with the shortest path for various network
    sizes.

//Clear display and environment variables

clc;
clear all;

//Creating a random topology which is tiny in size
    variable3 = 1;
    variable2 = 1;
for nodes=10:10:160
    b(variable3) = nodes;
    net_square_area=1000;              //network square area size is
        1000
    locality_radius=100;           //locality radius is 100

//   networkname = "Routing using DFS Algorithm";
    [g]=NL_T_LocalityConnex(nodes,net_square_area,
        locality_radius); //generation of a random topology in
        respect with the Locality method.

    variable1=NL_F_RandInt1n(length(g.node_x)); //selection of
        the source node
    window_index=1;              //window index
    g.node_diam(variable1)=40; //node diameter
    g.node_border(variable1)=10; //node border
    g.node_color(variable1)=5; //node color
    [f]=NL_G_ShowGraphN(g,window_index);//graph visualization

//Application of the DFS algorithm
    for variable1 = 1:5            //Run 5 iterations
        timer();             //Initialize timer
        [dist,pred]=NL_R_DFS(g,variable1); //application of
            NL_R_DFS
        A(variable1) = timer()      //Store timer value in array
```

```
      end
      average_time(variable2)=mean(A);         //Calculate average
         time taken
      disp(average_time(variable2),nodes,"Time of finding the
         shortest path for nodes",) //Display average time
      variable2 = variable2+1;
      variable3 = variable3+1;
end
clf();
for x = average_time
   for y = b
      disp('Time of Computation for DFS Algorithm')
      disp('Nodes')
      disp(y);
      disp('Time for Execution (Respectively)');
      disp(x);
      plot(b,average_time,'--mo');
      xtitle( 'Time of Computation for DFS Algorithm', 'Number
         of Nodes', 'Time', boxed = %t );
   end
end
```

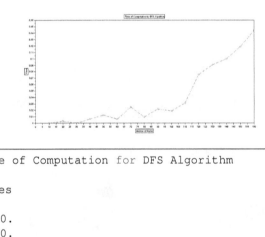

```
Time of Computation for DFS Algorithm

Nodes

   10.
   20.
   30.
   40.
   50.
   60.
   70.
   80.
   90.
   100.
   110.
   120.
   130.
```

```
140.
150.
160.
```

Time for Execution (Respectively)

```
0.
0.003125
0.
0.00625
0.0125
0.00625
0.025
0.009375
0.021875
0.01875
0.03125
0.075
0.090625
0.1
0.11875
0.14375
```

2.45 DFS Weight Comparison

```
//Authors:

//School of Computing Science and Engineering
//VIT Chennai

//Code to compute the CPU time taken by the DFSWeight routing
    algorithm to return the
//Vector of the total distance between each network node and
    the source node and
//Vector composed by the predecessor of each node in order to
    reach the source
//node in respect with the shortest path for various network
    sizes.

//Clear display and environment variables
clc
clear all

//Creating a random topology which is tiny in size
network_size=80;             //network size is 80
net_square_area=1000;              //network square area side is
    1000
locality_radius=100;         //locality radius is 100
[g]=NL_T_LocalityConnex(network_size,net_square_area,
    locality_radius); //generation of a random topology in
    respect with the Locality method.
iteration=NL_F_RandInt1n(length(g.node_x)); //selection of the
    source node
ind=1;                  //window index
g.node_diam(iteration)=40; //node diameter
g.node_border(iteration)=10; //node border
g.node_color(iteration)=5; //node color
[f]=NL_G_ShowGraphN(g,ind);//graph visualization
//Application of the DFSWeight algorithm
for iteration = 1:30          //Run 30 iterations
    timer();             //Initialize timer
    [dist,pred]=NL_R_DFSWeight(g,iteration); //application of
        NL_R_DFSWeight
    A(iteration) = timer()     //Store timer value in array
end
average_time=mean(A);               //Calculate average time taken
disp(average_time,"Tiny:")     //Display average time


//Creating a random topology which is small in size
network_size=90;
ind=2;                  //network size is 90
```

```
[g]=NL_T_LocalityConnex(network_size,net_square_area,
    locality_radius); //generation of a random topology in
    respect with the Locality method.
iteration=NL_F_RandInt1n(length(g.node_x)); //selection of the
    source node
g.node_diam(iteration)=40; //node diameter
g.node_border(iteration)=10; //node border
g.node_color(iteration)=5; //node color
[f]=NL_G_ShowGraphN(g,ind);//graph visualization
//Application of the DFSWeight algorithm
for iteration = 1:30          //Run 30 iterations
    timer();                  //Initialize timer
    [dist,pred]=NL_R_DFSWeight(g,iteration); //application of
        NL_R_DFSWeight
    A(iteration) = timer()    //Store timer value in array
end
average_time=mean(A);         //Calculate average time taken
disp(average_time,"Small:")   //Display average time


//Creating a random topology which is medium in size
network_size=120;             //network size is 120
ind=3;
[g]=NL_T_LocalityConnex(network_size,net_square_area,
    locality_radius); //generation of a random topology in
    respect with the Locality method.
iteration=NL_F_RandInt1n(length(g.node_x)); //selection of the
    source node
g.node_diam(iteration)=40; //node diameter
g.node_border(iteration)=10; //node border
g.node_color(iteration)=5; //node color
[f]=NL_G_ShowGraphN(g,ind);//graph visualization
//Application of the DFSWeight algorithm
for iteration = 1:30          //Run 30 iterations
    timer();                  //Initialize timer
    [dist,pred]=NL_R_DFSWeight(g,iteration); //application of
        NL_R_DFSWeight
    A(iteration) = timer()    //Store timer value in array
end
average_time=mean(A);         //Calculate average time taken
disp(average_time,"Medium:")  //Display average time


//Creating a random topology which is large in size
network_size=150;
ind=4;                        //network size is 150
[g]=NL_T_LocalityConnex(network_size,net_square_area,
    locality_radius); //generation of a random topology in
    respect with the Locality method.
```

```
iteration=NL_F_RandInt1n(length(g.node_x)); //selection of the
    source node
g.node_diam(iteration)=40; //node diameter
g.node_border(iteration)=10; //node border
g.node_color(iteration)=5; //node color
[f]=NL_G_ShowGraphN(g,ind);//graph visualization
//Application of the DFSWeight algorithm
for iteration = 1:30          //Run 30 iterations
    timer();              //Initialize timer
    [dist,pred]=NL_R_DFSWeight(g,iteration); //application of
        NL_R_DFSWeight
    A(iteration) = timer()      //Store timer value in array
end
average_time=mean(A);            //Calculate average time taken
disp(average_time,"Large:")      //Display average time


//Creating a random topology which is very large in size
network_size=180;
ind=5;              //network size is 180
[g]=NL_T_LocalityConnex(network_size,net_square_area,
    locality_radius); //generation of a random topology in
    respect with the Locality method.
iteration=NL_F_RandInt1n(length(g.node_x)); //selection of the
    source node
g.node_diam(iteration)=40; //node diameter
g.node_border(iteration)=10; //node border
g.node_color(iteration)=5; //node color
[f]=NL_G_ShowGraphN(g,ind);//graph visualization
//Application of the DFSWeight algorithm
for iteration = 1:30          //Run 30 iterations
    timer();              //Initialize timer
    [dist,pred]=NL_R_DFSWeight(g,iteration); //application of
        NL_R_DFSWeight
    A(iteration) = timer()      //Store timer value in array
end
average_time=mean(A);            //Calculate average time taken
disp(average_time,"Very Large:")     //Display average time
```

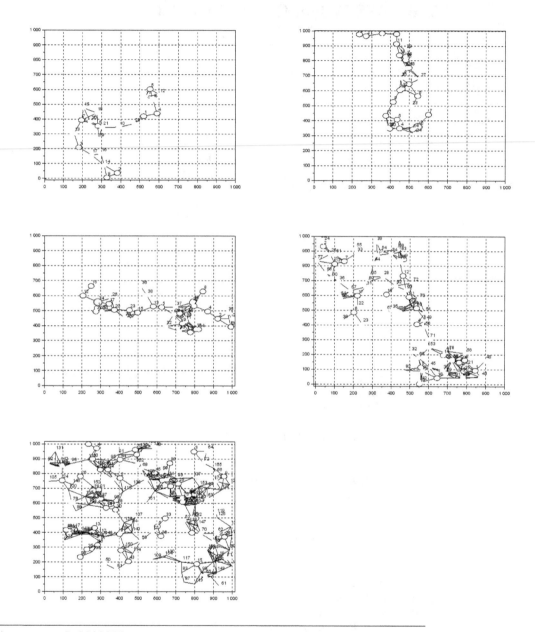

```
Tiny       :    0.0098958
Small      :    0.0041667
Medium     :    0.0223958
Large      :    0.05
Very Large :    0.0989583
```

2.46   DFS Weight Comparison Plot

```
//Authors:

//School of Computing Science and Engineering
//VIT Chennai

//Code to compute the CPU time taken by the DFSWeight routing
    algorithm to return the
//Vector of the total distance between each network node and
    the source node and
//Vector composed by the predecessor of each node in order to
    reach the source
//node in respect with the shortest path for various network
    sizes.

//Clear display and environment variables

clc;
clear all;

//Creating a random topology which is tiny in size
    variable3 = 1;
    variable2 = 1;
for nodes=10:10:160
    b(variable3) = nodes;
    net_square_area=1000;              //network square area size is
        1000
    locality_radius=100;          //locality radius is 100

//   networkname = "Routing using DFSWeight Algorithm";
    [g]=NL_T_LocalityConnex(nodes,net_square_area,
        locality_radius); //generation of a random topology in
        respect with the Locality method.

    variable1=NL_F_RandInt1n(length(g.node_x)); //selection of
        the source node
    window_index=1;                //window index
    g.node_diam(variable1)=40; //node diameter
    g.node_border(variable1)=10; //node border
    g.node_color(variable1)=5; //node color
    [f]=NL_G_ShowGraphN(g,window_index);//graph visualization

//Application of the DFSWeight algorithm
    for variable1 = 1:5            //Run 5 iterations
        timer();              //Initialize timer
        [dist,pred]=NL_R_DFSWeight(g,variable1); //application of
            NL_R_DFSWeight
        A(variable1) = timer()      //Store timer value in array
```

```
    end
    average_time(variable2)=mean(A);          //Calculate average
        time taken
    disp(average_time(variable2),nodes,"Time of finding the
        shortest path for nodes",) //Display average time
    variable2 = variable2+1;
    variable3 = variable3+1;
end
clf();
for x = average_time
    for y = b
        disp('Time of Computation for DFSWeight Algorithm')
        disp('Nodes')
        disp(y);
        disp('Time for Execution (Respectively)');
        disp(x);
        plot(b,average_time,'--mo');
        xtitle( 'Time of Computation for DFSWeight Algorithm', '
            Number of Nodes', 'Time', boxed = %t );
    end
end
```

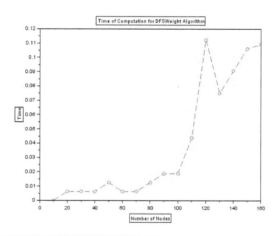

```
Time of Computation for DFSWeight Algorithm

Nodes

    10.
    20.
    30.
    40.
    50.
    60.
    70.
```

```
80.
90.
100.
110.
120.
130.
140.
150.
160.
```

Time for Execution (Respectively)

```
0.
0.00625
0.00625
0.00625
0.0125
0.00625
0.00625
0.0125
0.01875
0.01875
0.04375
0.1125
0.075
0.090625
0.10625
0.109375
```

2.47   Dijikstra Comparison Plot

```
//Authors:

//School of Computing Science and Engineering
//VIT Chennai

//Code to compute the CPU time taken by the Dijkstra routing
   algorithm to return the
//Vector of the total distance between each network node and
   the source node and
//Vector composed by the predecessor of each node in order to
   reach the source
//node in respect with the shortest path for various network
   sizes.

//Clear display and environment variables

clc;
clear all;

//Creating a random topology which is tiny in size
   variable3 = 1;
   variable2 = 1;
for nodes=10:10:160
   b(variable3) = nodes;
   net_square_area=1000;           //network square area size is
      1000
   locality_radius=100;            //locality radius is 100

//    networkname = "Routing using Dijkstra Algorithm";
   [g]=NL_T_LocalityConnex(nodes,net_square_area,
      locality_radius); //generation of a random topology in
      respect with the Locality method.

   variable1=NL_F_RandInt1n(length(g.node_x)); //selection of
      the source node
   window_index=1;                  //window index
   g.node_diam(variable1)=40; //node diameter
   g.node_border(variable1)=10; //node border
   g.node_color(variable1)=5; //node color
   [f]=NL_G_ShowGraphN(g,window_index);//graph visualization

//Application of the Dijkstra algorithm
   for variable1 = 1:5              //Run 5 iterations
      timer();             //Initialize timer
      [dist,pred]=NL_R_Dijkstra(g,variable1); //application of
         NL_R_Dijkstra
      A(variable1) = timer()      //Store timer value in array
```

```
    end
    average_time(variable2)=mean(A);          //Calculate average
        time taken
    disp(average_time(variable2),nodes,"Time of finding the
        shortest path for nodes",) //Display average time
    variable2 = variable2+1;
    variable3 = variable3+1;
end
clf();
for x = average_time
    for y = b
        disp('Time of Computation for Dijkstra Algorithm')
        disp('Nodes')
        disp(y);
        disp('Time for Execution (Respectively)');
        disp(x);
        plot(b,average_time,'--mo');
        xtitle( 'Time of Computation for Dijkstra Algorithm', '
            Number of Nodes', 'Time', boxed = %t );
    end
end
```

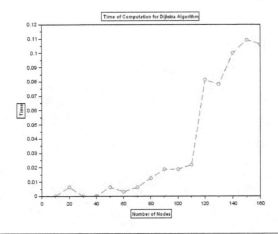

```
Time of Computation for Dijkstra Algorithm

Nodes

    10.
    20.
    30.
    40.
    50.
    60.
    70.
```

```
80.
90.
100.
110.
120.
130.
140.
150.
160.
```

Time for Execution (Respectively)

```
0.
0.00625
0.
0.
0.00625
0.003125
0.00625
0.0125
0.01875
0.01875
0.021875
0.08125
0.078125
0.1
0.109375
0.10625
```

2.48 Dijkstra Comparison

```
//Authors:

//School of Computing Science and Engineering
//VIT Chennai

//Code to compute the CPU time taken by the Dijkstra routing
    algorithm to return the
//Vector of the total distance between each network node and
    the source node and
//Vector composed by the predecessor of each node in order to
    reach the source
//node in respect with the shortest path for various network
    sizes.

//Clear display and environment variables
clc
clear all

//Creating a random topology which is tiny in size
network_size=80;              //network size is 80
net_square_area=1000;            //network square area side is
    1000
locality_radius=100;          //locality radius is 100
[g]=NL_T_LocalityConnex(network_size,net_square_area,
    locality_radius); //generation of a random topology in
    respect with the Locality method.
iteration=NL_F_RandInt1n(length(g.node_x)); //selection of the
    source node
ind=1;                 //window index
g.node_diam(iteration)=40; //node diameter
g.node_border(iteration)=10; //node border
g.node_color(iteration)=5; //node color
[f]=NL_G_ShowGraphN(g,ind);//graph visualization
//Application of the Dijkstra algorithm
for iteration = 1:30          //Run 30 iterations
    timer();          //Initialize timer
    [dist,pred]=NL_R_Dijkstra(g,iteration); //application of
        NL_R_Dijkstra
    A(iteration) = timer()     //Store timer value in array
end
average_time=mean(A);            //Calculate average time taken
disp(average_time,"Tiny:")     //Display average time


//Creating a random topology which is small in size
ind=2;
network_size=90;            //network size is 90
```

```
[g]=NL_T_LocalityConnex(network_size,net_square_area,
    locality_radius); //generation of a random topology in
    respect with the Locality method.
iteration=NL_F_RandInt1n(length(g.node_x)); //selection of the
    source node
g.node_diam(iteration)=40; //node diameter
g.node_border(iteration)=10; //node border
g.node_color(iteration)=5; //node color
[f]=NL_G_ShowGraphN(g,ind);//graph visualization
//Application of the Dijkstra algorithm
for iteration = 1:30          //Run 30 iterations
    timer();              //Initialize timer
    [dist,pred]=NL_R_Dijkstra(g,iteration); //application of
        NL_R_Dijkstra
    A(iteration) = timer()     //Store timer value in array
end
average_time=mean(A);          //Calculate average time taken
disp(average_time,"Small:")      //Display average time


//Creating a random topology which is medium in size
ind=3;
network_size=120;              //network size is 120
[g]=NL_T_LocalityConnex(network_size,net_square_area,
    locality_radius); //generation of a random topology in
    respect with the Locality method.
iteration=NL_F_RandInt1n(length(g.node_x)); //selection of the
    source node
g.node_diam(iteration)=40; //node diameter
g.node_border(iteration)=10; //node border
g.node_color(iteration)=5; //node color
[f]=NL_G_ShowGraphN(g,ind);//graph visualization
//Application of the Dijkstra algorithm
for iteration = 1:30          //Run 30 iterations
    timer();              //Initialize timer
    [dist,pred]=NL_R_Dijkstra(g,iteration); //application of
        NL_R_Dijkstra
    A(iteration) = timer()     //Store timer value in array
end
average_time=mean(A);          //Calculate average time taken
disp(average_time,"Medium:")      //Display average time


//Creating a random topology which is large in size
ind=4;
network_size=150;              //network size is 150
[g]=NL_T_LocalityConnex(network_size,net_square_area,
    locality_radius); //generation of a random topology in
    respect with the Locality method.
```

```
iteration=NL_F_RandInt1n(length(g.node_x)); //selection of the
   source node
g.node_diam(iteration)=40; //node diameter
g.node_border(iteration)=10; //node border
g.node_color(iteration)=5; //node color
[f]=NL_G_ShowGraphN(g,ind);//graph visualization
//Application of the Dijkstra algorithm
for iteration = 1:30            //Run 30 iterations
   timer();                //Initialize timer
   [dist,pred]=NL_R_Dijkstra(g,iteration); //application of
      NL_R_Dijkstra
   A(iteration) = timer()       //Store timer value in array
end
average_time=mean(A);               //Calculate average time taken
disp(average_time,"Large:")         //Display average time


//Creating a random topology which is very large in size
ind=5;
network_size=180;               //network size is 180
[g]=NL_T_LocalityConnex(network_size,net_square_area,
   locality_radius); //generation of a random topology in
   respect with the Locality method.
iteration=NL_F_RandInt1n(length(g.node_x)); //selection of the
   source node
g.node_diam(iteration)=40; //node diameter
g.node_border(iteration)=10; //node border
g.node_color(iteration)=5; //node color
[f]=NL_G_ShowGraphN(g,ind);//graph visualization
//Application of the Dijkstra algorithm
for iteration = 1:30            //Run 30 iterations
   timer();                //Initialize timer
   [dist,pred]=NL_R_Dijkstra(g,iteration); //application of
      NL_R_Dijkstra
   A(iteration) = timer()       //Store timer value in array
end
average_time=mean(A);               //Calculate average time taken
disp(average_time,"Very Large:")      //Display average time
```

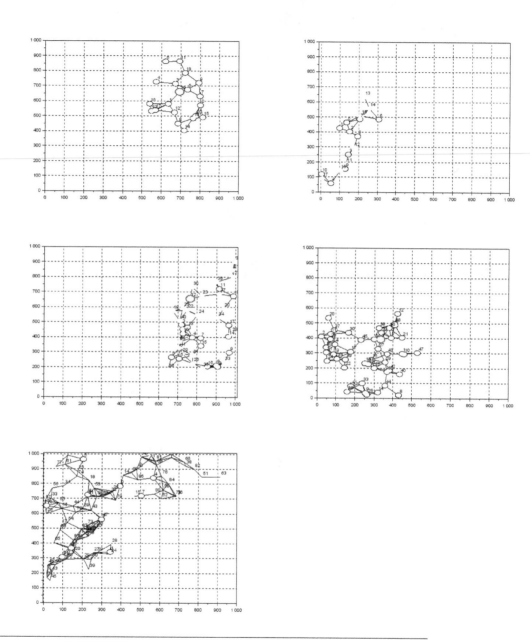

```
Tiny       :   0.0083333
Small      :   0.0083333
Medium     :   0.0223958
Large      :   0.0255208
Very Large :   0.0520833
```

2.49 FloydWarshall Comparison

```
//Authors:

//School of Computing Science and Engineering
//VIT Chennai

//Code to compute the CPU time taken by the FloydWarshall
    routing algorithm to return the
//Vector of the total distance between each network node and
    the source node and
//Vector composed by the predecessor of each node in order to
    reach the source
//node in respect with the shortest path for various network
    sizes.

//Clear display and environment variables
clc
clear all

//Creating a random topology which is tiny in size
network_size=80;            //network size is 80
net_square_area=1000;           //network square area side is
    1000
locality_radius=100;        //locality radius is 100
[g]=NL_T_LocalityConnex(network_size,net_square_area,
    locality_radius); //generation of a random topology in
    respect with the Locality method.
window_index=1;             //window index
g.node_diam(iteration)=40; //node diameter
g.node_border(iteration)=10; //node border
g.node_color(iteration)=5; //node color
[f]=NL_G_ShowGraphN(g,window_index);//graph visualization
//Application of the FloydWarshall algorithm
for iteration = 1:5         //Run 5 iterations
    timer();            //Initialize timer
    [dist,pred]=NL_R_FloydWarshall(g); //application of
        NL_R_FloydWarshall
    A(iteration) = timer()      //Store timer value in array
end
average_time=mean(A);           //Calculate average time taken
disp(average_time,"Tiny:")      //Display average time


//Creating a random topology which is small in size
network_size=90;            //network size is 90
window_index=2;
[g]=NL_T_LocalityConnex(network_size,net_square_area,
    locality_radius); //generation of a random topology in
```

```
    respect with the Locality method.
g.node_diam(iteration)=40; //node diameter
g.node_border(iteration)=10; //node border
g.node_color(iteration)=5; //node color
[f]=NL_G_ShowGraphN(g,window_index);//graph visualization
//Application of the FloydWarshall algorithm
for iteration = 1:5          //Run 5 iterations
    timer();                //Initialize timer
    [dist,pred]=NL_R_FloydWarshall(g); //application of
        NL_R_FloydWarshall
    A(iteration) = timer()     //Store timer value in array
end
average_time=mean(A);            //Calculate average time taken
disp(average_time,"Small:")      //Display average time


//Creating a random topology which is medium in size
window_index=3;
network_size=120;                //network size is 120
[g]=NL_T_LocalityConnex(network_size,net_square_area,
    locality_radius); //generation of a random topology in
    respect with the Locality method.
g.node_diam(iteration)=40; //node diameter
g.node_border(iteration)=10; //node border
g.node_color(iteration)=5; //node color
[f]=NL_G_ShowGraphN(g,window_index);//graph visualization
//Application of the FloydWarshall algorithm
for iteration = 1:5          //Run 5 iterations
    timer();                //Initialize timer
    [dist,pred]=NL_R_FloydWarshall(g); //application of
        NL_R_FloydWarshall
    A(iteration) = timer()     //Store timer value in array
end
average_time=mean(A);            //Calculate average time taken
disp(average_time,"Medium:")      //Display average time


//Creating a random topology which is large in size
window_index=4;
network_size=150;                //network size is 150
[g]=NL_T_LocalityConnex(network_size,net_square_area,
    locality_radius); //generation of a random topology in
    respect with the Locality method.
g.node_diam(iteration)=40; //node diameter
g.node_border(iteration)=10; //node border
g.node_color(iteration)=5; //node color
[f]=NL_G_ShowGraphN(g,window_index);//graph visualization
//Application of the FloydWarshall algorithm
for iteration = 1:5          //Run 5 iterations
    timer();                //Initialize timer
```

```
    [dist,pred]=NL_R_FloydWarshall(g); //application of
        NL_R_FloydWarshall
    A(iteration) = timer()        //Store timer value in array
end
average_time=mean(A);                  //Calculate average time taken
disp(average_time,"Large:")        //Display average time


//Creating a random topology which is very large in size
window_index=5;
network_size=180;              //network size is 180
[g]=NL_T_LocalityConnex(network_size,net_square_area,
    locality_radius); //generation of a random topology in
    respect with the Locality method.
g.node_diam(iteration)=40; //node diameter
g.node_border(iteration)=10; //node border
g.node_color(iteration)=5; //node color
[f]=NL_G_ShowGraphN(g,window_index);//graph visualization
//Application of the FloydWarshall algorithm
for iteration = 1:5            //Run 5 iterations
    timer();                //Initialize timer
    [dist,pred]=NL_R_FloydWarshall(g); //application of
        NL_R_FloydWarshall
    A(iteration) = timer()        //Store timer value in array
end
average_time=mean(A);                  //Calculate average time taken
disp(average_time,"Very Large:")     //Display average time
```

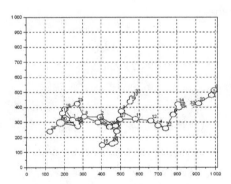 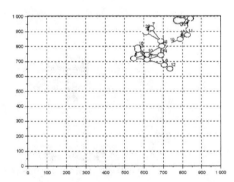

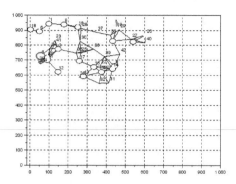
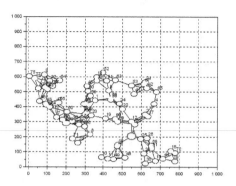
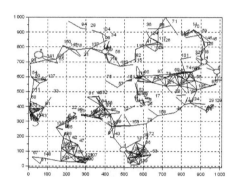

```
Tiny: 0.0536458
Small:  0.0442708
Medium: 0.0682292
Large:  0.2223958
Very Large: 1.5776042
```

2.50   FloydWarshall Comparison Plot

```
//Authors:

//School of Computing Science and Engineering
//VIT Chennai

//Code to compute the CPU time taken by the FloydWarshall
    routing algorithm to return the
//Vector of the total distance between each network node and
    the source node and
//Vector composed by the predecessor of each node in order to
    reach the source
//node in respect with the shortest path for various network
    sizes.

//Clear display and environment variables

clc;
clear all;

//Creating a random topology which is tiny in size
    variable3 = 1;
    variable2 = 1;
for nodes=10:10:160
    b(variable3) = nodes;
    net_square_area=1000;             //network square area side is
        1000
    locality_radius=100;             //locality radius is 100
//   networkname = "Routing using FloydWarshall Algorithm";
    [g]=NL_T_LocalityConnex(nodes,net_square_area,
        locality_radius); //generation of a random topology in
        respect with the Locality method.
    variable1=NL_F_RandInt1n(length(g.node_x)); //selection of
        the source node
    window_index=1;                   //window index
    g.node_diam(variable1)=40; //node diameter
    g.node_border(variable1)=10; //node border
    g.node_color(variable1)=5; //node color
    [f]=NL_G_ShowGraphN(g,window_index);//graph visualization
//Application of the FloydWarshall algorithm
    for variable1 = 1:5               //Run 5 iterations
        timer();              //Initialize timer
        [dist,pred]=NL_R_FloydWarshall(g); //application of
            NL_R_FloydWarshall
        A(variable1) = timer()     //Store timer value in array
    end
    average_time(variable2)=mean(A);         //Calculate average
        time taken
```

```
    disp(average_time(variable2),nodes,"Time of finding the
        shortest path for nodes",) //Display average time
    variable2 = variable2+1;
    variable3 = variable3+1;
end
clf();
for x = average_time
    for y = b
        disp('Time of Computation for FloydWarshall Algorithm')
        disp('Nodes')
        disp(y);
        disp('Time for Execution (Respectively)');
        disp(x);
        plot(b,average_time,'--mo');
        xtitle( 'Time of Computation for FloydWarshall Algorithm'
            , 'Number of Nodes', 'Time', boxed = %t );
    end
end
```

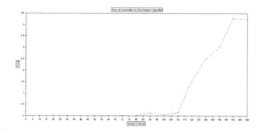

```
Time of Computation for FloydWarshall Algorithm

Nodes

    10.
    20.
    30.
    40.
    50.
    60.
    70.
    80.
    90.
    100.
    110.
    120.
    130.
    140.
    150.
    160.
```

```
Time for Execution (Respectively)

    0.00625
    0.
    0.
    0.
    0.
    0.
    0.0125
    0.003125
    0.121875
    0.053125
    0.140625
    1.528125
    2.5
    3.00625
    4.28125
    4.228125
```

2.51   Gigantic Network Routing Performance

```
//Code to compute the CPU time taken by each routing algorithm
    to return the
//Vector of the total distance between each network node and
    the source node and
//Vector composed by the predecessor of each node in order to
    reach the source
//node in respect with the shortest path.
//NOTE: Prim's Algorithm also returns Vector that gathers the
    chronological order
//how network nodes are visited. Refer to documentation for
    details.

//Clear display and environment variables
clc
clear all


disp("For a Gigantic Network Topology with Nodes in the network
    = 210 ");
//Creating a random topology which is Gigantic in size
network_size=210;            //network size is 210
net_square_area=1000;             //network square area side is
    1000
locality_radius=100;         //locality radius is 100
[g]=NL_T_LocalityConnex(network_size,net_square_area,
    locality_radius); //generation of a random topology in
    respect with the Locality method.
iteration=NL_F_RandInt1n(length(g.node_x)); //selection of the
    source node
window_index=1;              //window index
g.node_diam(iteration)=40; //node diameter
g.node_border(iteration)=10; //node border
g.node_color(iteration)=5; //node color
[f]=NL_G_ShowGraphN(g,window_index);//graph visualization

//Application of the BFS algorithm
for iteration = 1:10          //Run 10 iterations
    timer();            //Initialize timer
    [dist,pred]=NL_R_BFS(g,iteration); //application of NL_R_BFS
    A(iteration) = timer()     //Store timer value in array
end
average_time=mean(A);           //Calculate average time taken
disp(average_time,"BFS:")      //Display average time

//Application of the Weighted BFS algorithm
```

```
for iteration = 1:10
    timer();
    [dist,pred]=NL_R_BFSWeight(g,iteration);//application of
        NL_R_BFSWeight
    A(iteration) = timer()
end
average_time=mean(A);
disp(average_time, "Weighted BFS:")

//Application of the Bellman-Ford algorithm
for iteration = 1:10
    timer();
    [dist,pred]=NL_R_BellmanFord(g,iteration);//application of
        NL_R_BellmanFord
    A(iteration) = timer()
end
average_time=mean(A);
disp(average_time,"Bellman-Ford:")

//Application of the DFS algorithm
for iteration = 1:10
    timer();
    [dist,pred]=NL_R_DFS(g,iteration);//application of NL_R_DFS
    A(iteration) = timer()
end
average_time=mean(A);
disp(average_time,"DFS:")

//Application of the Weighted DFS algorithm
for iteration = 1:10
    timer();
    [dist,pred]=NL_R_DFSWeight(g,iteration);//application of
        NL_R_DFSWeight
    A(iteration) = timer()
end
average_time=mean(A);
disp(average_time,"Weighted DFS:")

//Application of the Dijkstra algorithm
for iteration = 1:10
    timer();
    [dist,pred]=NL_R_Dijkstra(g,iteration);//application of
        NL_R_Dijkstra
    A(iteration) = timer()
end
average_time=mean(A);
disp(average_time,"Dijkstra:")

//Application of the Floyd-Warshall algorithm
for iteration = 1:10
```

```
   timer();
   [dist,pred]=NL_R_FloydWarshall(g);//application of
      NL_R_FloydWarshall
   A(iteration) = timer()
end
average_time=mean(A);
disp(average_time,"Floyd-Warshall:")

//Application of the Prim's algorithm
for iteration = 1:10
   timer();
   [dist,v,pred]=NL_R_Prim(g,iteration,2,1);//application of
      NL_R_Prim, setting Display Parameter as 2 and window
      index as 1
   A(iteration) = timer()
end
average_time=mean(A);
disp(average_time,"Prim:")
```

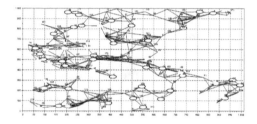 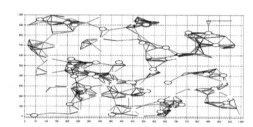

```
 For a Gigantic Network Topology with Nodes in the network = 210
BFS    : 0.18125
Weighted BFS : 0.0953125
Bellman-Ford : 1.85
DFS    : 0.09375
Weighted DFS : 0.0859375
Dijkstra : 0.15625
Floyd-Warshall  : 21.207812
Prim   : 7.0078125
```

2.52   Large Network Routing Performance

```
//Code to compute the CPU time taken by each routing algorithm
    to return the
//Vector of the total distance between each network node and
    the source node and
//Vector composed by the predecessor of each node in order to
    reach the source
//node in respect with the shortest path.
//NOTE: Prim's Algorithm also returns Vector that gathers the
    chronological order
//how network nodes are visited. Refer to documentation for
    details.

//Clear display and environment variables
clc
clear all


disp("For a Large Network Topology with Nodes in the network =
    150 ");
//Creating a random topology which is Large in size
network_size=150;              //network size is 150
net_square_area=1000;             //network square area side is
    1000
locality_radius=100;           //locality radius is 100
[g]=NL_T_LocalityConnex(network_size,net_square_area,
    locality_radius); //generation of a random topology in
    respect with the Locality method.
iteration=NL_F_RandInt1n(length(g.node_x)); //selection of the
    source node
window_index=1;                 //window index
g.node_diam(iteration)=40; //node diameter
g.node_border(iteration)=10; //node border
g.node_color(iteration)=5; //node color
[f]=NL_G_ShowGraphN(g,window_index);//graph visualization

//Application of the BFS algorithm
for iteration = 1:10               //Run 10 iterations
   timer();              //Initialize timer
   [dist,pred]=NL_R_BFS(g,iteration); //application of NL_R_BFS
   A(iteration) = timer()      //Store timer value in array
end
average_time=mean(A);              //Calculate average time taken
disp(average_time,"BFS:")        //Display average time

//Application of the Weighted BFS algorithm
```

```
for iteration = 1:10
    timer();
    [dist,pred]=NL_R_BFSWeight(g,iteration);//application of
        NL_R_BFSWeight
    A(iteration) = timer()
end
average_time=mean(A);
disp(average_time, "Weighted BFS:")

//Application of the Bellman-Ford algorithm
for iteration = 1:10
    timer();
    [dist,pred]=NL_R_BellmanFord(g,iteration);//application of
        NL_R_BellmanFord
    A(iteration) = timer()
end
average_time=mean(A);
disp(average_time,"Bellman-Ford:")

//Application of the DFS algorithm
for iteration = 1:10
    timer();
    [dist,pred]=NL_R_DFS(g,iteration);//application of NL_R_DFS
    A(iteration) = timer()
end
average_time=mean(A);
disp(average_time,"DFS:")

//Application of the Weighted DFS algorithm
for iteration = 1:10
    timer();
    [dist,pred]=NL_R_DFSWeight(g,iteration);//application of
        NL_R_DFSWeight
    A(iteration) = timer()
end
average_time=mean(A);
disp(average_time,"Weighted DFS:")

//Application of the Dijkstra algorithm
for iteration = 1:10
    timer();
    [dist,pred]=NL_R_Dijkstra(g,iteration);//application of
        NL_R_Dijkstra
    A(iteration) = timer()
end
average_time=mean(A);
disp(average_time,"Dijkstra:")

//Application of the Floyd-Warshall algorithm
for iteration = 1:10
```

```
    timer();
    [dist,pred]=NL_R_FloydWarshall(g);//application of
        NL_R_FloydWarshall
    A(iteration) = timer()
end
average_time=mean(A);
disp(average_time,"Floyd-Warshall:")

//Application of the Prim's algorithm
for iteration = 1:10
    timer();
    [dist,v,pred]=NL_R_Prim(g,iteration,2,1);//application of
        NL_R_Prim, setting Display Parameter as 2 and window
        index as 1
    A(iteration) = timer()
end
average_time=mean(A);
disp(average_time,"Prim:")
```

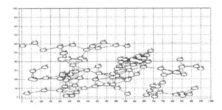
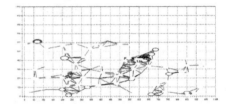
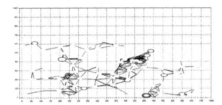

```
For a Large Network Topology with Nodes in the network = 150

BFS     : 0.1234375
Weighted BFS : 0.065625
Bellman-Ford : 0.3734375
DFS     : 0.0421875
Weighted DFS : 0.053125
Dijkstra : 0.05625
Floyd-Warshall  : 2.0625
Prim    : 2.20625
```

2.53   Medium Network Routing Performance

```
//Code to compute the CPU time taken by each routing algorithm
    to return the
//Vector of the total distance between each network node and
    the source node and
//Vector composed by the predecessor of each node in order to
    reach the source
//node in respect with the shortest path.
//NOTE: Prim's Algorithm also returns Vector that gathers the
    chronological order
//how network nodes are visited. Refer to documentation for
    details.

//Clear display and environment variables
clc
clear all


disp("For a Medium Network Topology with Nodes in the network =
    120 ");
//Creating a random topology which is Medium in size
network_size=120;              //network size is 120
net_square_area=1000;            //network square area side is
    1000
locality_radius=100;           //locality radius is 100
[g]=NL_T_LocalityConnex(network_size,net_square_area,
    locality_radius); //generation of a random topology in
    respect with the Locality method.
iteration=NL_F_RandInt1n(length(g.node_x)); //selection of the
    source node
window_index=1;              //window index
g.node_diam(iteration)=40; //node diameter
g.node_border(iteration)=10; //node border
g.node_color(iteration)=5; //node color
[f]=NL_G_ShowGraphN(g,window_index);//graph visualization

//Application of the BFS algorithm
for iteration = 1:10             //Run 10 iterations
   timer();            //Initialize timer
   [dist,pred]=NL_R_BFS(g,iteration); //application of NL_R_BFS
   A(iteration) = timer()      //Store timer value in array
end
average_time=mean(A);              //Calculate average time taken
disp(average_time,"BFS:")        //Display average time

//Application of the Weighted BFS algorithm
```

```
for iteration = 1:10
    timer();
    [dist,pred]=NL_R_BFSWeight(g,iteration);//application of
        NL_R_BFSWeight
    A(iteration) = timer()
end
average_time=mean(A);
disp(average_time, "Weighted BFS:")

//Application of the Bellman-Ford algorithm
for iteration = 1:10
    timer();
    [dist,pred]=NL_R_BellmanFord(g,iteration);//application of
        NL_R_BellmanFord
    A(iteration) = timer()
end
average_time=mean(A);
disp(average_time,"Bellman-Ford:")

//Application of the DFS algorithm
for iteration = 1:10
    timer();
    [dist,pred]=NL_R_DFS(g,iteration);//application of NL_R_DFS
    A(iteration) = timer()
end
average_time=mean(A);
disp(average_time,"DFS:")

//Application of the Weighted DFS algorithm
for iteration = 1:10
    timer();
    [dist,pred]=NL_R_DFSWeight(g,iteration);//application of
        NL_R_DFSWeight
    A(iteration) = timer()
end
average_time=mean(A);
disp(average_time,"Weighted DFS:")

//Application of the Dijkstra algorithm
for iteration = 1:10
    timer();
    [dist,pred]=NL_R_Dijkstra(g,iteration);//application of
        NL_R_Dijkstra
    A(iteration) = timer()
end
average_time=mean(A);
disp(average_time,"Dijkstra:")

//Application of the Floyd-Warshall algorithm
for iteration = 1:10
```

```
   timer();
   [dist,pred]=NL_R_FloydWarshall(g);//application of
      NL_R_FloydWarshall
   A(iteration) = timer()
end
average_time=mean(A);
disp(average_time,"Floyd-Warshall:")

//Application of the Prim's algorithm
for iteration = 1:10
   timer();
   [dist,v,pred]=NL_R_Prim(g,iteration,2,1);//application of
      NL_R_Prim, setting Display Parameter as 2 and window
      index as 1
   A(iteration) = timer()
end
average_time=mean(A);
disp(average_time,"Prim:")
```

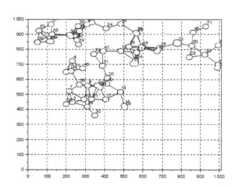 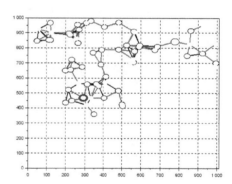

```
For a Medium Network Topology with Nodes in the network = 120

 BFS     : 0.059375
Weighted BFS : 0.040625
Bellman-Ford : 0.1109375
DFS      : 0.0328125
Weighted DFS : 0.0484375
Dijkstra : 0.028125
Floyd-Warshall  : 0.5875
Prim     : 1.171875
```

2.54 Prims Comparison

```
//Code to compute the CPU time taken by the Prim routing
    algorithm to return the
//Vector of the total distance between each network node and
    the source node and
//Vector composed by the predecessor of each node in order to
    reach the source
//node in respect with the shortest path for various network
    sizes.

//Clear display and environment variables
clc
clear all

//Creating a random topology which is tiny in size
network_size=80;              //network size is 80
net_square_area=1000;             //network square area side is
    1000
locality_radius=100;          //locality radius is 100
[g]=NL_T_LocalityConnex(network_size,net_square_area,
    locality_radius); //generation of a random topology in
    respect with the Locality method.
iteration=NL_F_RandInt1n(length(g.node_x)); //selection of the
    source node
window_index=1;               //window index
g.node_diam(iteration)=40; //node diameter
g.node_border(iteration)=10; //node border
g.node_color(iteration)=5; //node color
[f]=NL_G_ShowGraphN(g,window_index);//graph visualization
//Application of the Prim algorithm
for iteration = 1:10          //Run 10 iterations
   timer();                //Initialize timer
   [dist,v,pred]=NL_R_Prim(g,iteration,2,1); //application of
       NL_R_Prim
   A(iteration) = timer()     //Store timer value in array
end
average_time=mean(A);              //Calculate average time taken
disp(average_time,"Tiny:")        //Display average time


//Creating a random topology which is small in size
network_size=90;              //network size is 90
[g]=NL_T_LocalityConnex(network_size,net_square_area,
    locality_radius); //generation of a random topology in
    respect with the Locality method.
```

```
iteration=NL_F_RandInt1n(length(g.node_x)); //selection of the
    source node
g.node_diam(iteration)=40; //node diameter
g.node_border(iteration)=10; //node border
g.node_color(iteration)=5; //node color
window_index=2;               //window index
[f]=NL_G_ShowGraphN(g,window_index);//graph visualization
//Application of the Prim algorithm
for iteration = 1:10              //Run 10 iterations
    timer();                    //Initialize timer
    [dist,v,pred]=NL_R_Prim(g,iteration,2,1); //application of
        NL_R_Prim
    A(iteration) = timer()      //Store timer value in array
end
average_time=mean(A);               //Calculate average time taken
disp(average_time,"Small:")       //Display average time


//Creating a random topology which is medium in size
network_size=120;              //network size is 120
[g]=NL_T_LocalityConnex(network_size,net_square_area,
    locality_radius); //generation of a random topology in
    respect with the Locality method.
iteration=NL_F_RandInt1n(length(g.node_x)); //selection of the
    source node
window_index=3;                 //window index
g.node_diam(iteration)=40; //node diameter
g.node_border(iteration)=10; //node border
g.node_color(iteration)=5; //node color
[f]=NL_G_ShowGraphN(g,window_index);//graph visualization
//Application of the Prim algorithm
for iteration = 1:10              //Run 10 iterations
    timer();               //Initialize timer
    [dist,v,pred]=NL_R_Prim(g,iteration,2,1); //application of
        NL_R_Prim
    A(iteration) = timer()      //Store timer value in array
end
average_time=mean(A);               //Calculate average time taken
disp(average_time,"Medium:")       //Display average time


//Creating a random topology which is large in size
network_size=150;               //network size is 150
[g]=NL_T_LocalityConnex(network_size,net_square_area,
    locality_radius); //generation of a random topology in
    respect with the Locality method.
iteration=NL_F_RandInt1n(length(g.node_x)); //selection of the
    source node
window_index=4;                 //window index
g.node_diam(iteration)=40; //node diameter
```

```
g.node_border(iteration)=10; //node border
g.node_color(iteration)=5; //node color
[f]=NL_G_ShowGraphN(g,window_index);//graph visualization
//Application of the Prim algorithm
for iteration = 1:10            //Run 10 iterations
    timer();                //Initialize timer
    [dist,v,pred]=NL_R_Prim(g,iteration,2,1); //application of
        NL_R_Prim
    A(iteration) = timer()       //Store timer value in array
end
average_time=mean(A);             //Calculate average time taken
disp(average_time,"Large:")       //Display average time


//Creating a random topology which is very large in size
network_size=180;                 //network size is 180
[g]=NL_T_LocalityConnex(network_size,net_square_area,
    locality_radius); //generation of a random topology in
    respect with the Locality method.
iteration=NL_F_RandInt1n(length(g.node_x)); //selection of the
    source node
window_index=5;                   //window index
g.node_diam(iteration)=40; //node diameter
g.node_border(iteration)=10; //node border
g.node_color(iteration)=5; //node color
[f]=NL_G_ShowGraphN(g,window_index);//graph visualization
//Application of the Prim algorithm
for iteration = 1:10            //Run 10 iterations
    timer();                //Initialize timer
    [dist,v,pred]=NL_R_Prim(g,iteration,2,1); //application of
        NL_R_Prim
    A(iteration) = timer()       //Store timer value in array
end
average_time=mean(A);             //Calculate average time taken
disp(average_time,"Very Large:")     //Display average time
```

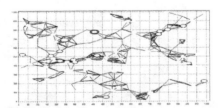
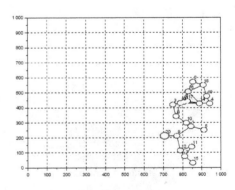

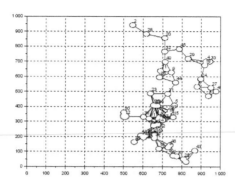

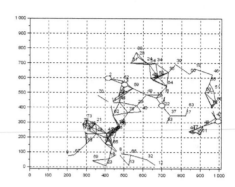

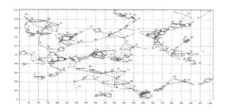

```
Tiny       : 0.5375
Small      : 0.4140625
Medium     : 1.0578125
Large      : 1.278125
Very Large : 3.4203125
```

2.55   Prims Comparison Plot

```
//Code to compute the CPU time taken by the Prim's routing
    algorithm to return the
//Vector of the total distance between each network node and
    the source node and
//Vector composed by the predecessor of each node in order to
    reach the source
//node in respect with the shortest path for various network
    sizes.

//Clear display and environment variables

clc;
clear all;

//Creating a random topology which is tiny in size
    variable3 = 1;
    variable2 = 1;
for nodes=10:10:160
    b(variable3) = nodes;
    net_square_area=1000;            //network square area side is
        1000
    locality_radius=100;            //locality radius is 100
//   networkname = "Routing using Prim Algorithm";
    [g]=NL_T_LocalityConnex(nodes,net_square_area,
        locality_radius); //generation of a random topology in
        respect with the Locality method.
    variable1=NL_F_RandInt1n(length(g.node_x)); //selection of
        the source node
    window_index=1;                 //window index
    g.node_diam(variable1)=40; //node diameter
    g.node_border(variable1)=10; //node border
    g.node_color(variable1)=5; //node color
    [f]=NL_G_ShowGraphN(g,window_index);//graph visualization
//Application of the Prim algorithm
    for variable1 = 1:2              //Run 2 iterations
        timer();                //Initialize timer
        [dist,s,pred]=NL_R_Prim(g,variable1,2,1); //application
            of NL_R_Prim
        A(variable1) = timer()     //Store timer value in array
    end
    average_time(variable2)=mean(A);          //Calculate average
        time taken
    disp(average_time(variable2),nodes,"Time of finding the
        shortest path for nodes") //Display average time
    variable2 = variable2+1;
```

```
      variable3 = variable3+1;
end
clf();
for x = average_time
   for y = b
      disp('Time of Computation for Prim Algorithm')
      disp('Nodes')
      disp(y);
      disp('Time for Execution (Respectively)');
      disp(x);
      plot(b,average_time,'--mo');
      xtitle( 'Time of Computation for Prim Algorithm', 'Number
         of Nodes', 'Time', boxed = %t );
   end
end
```

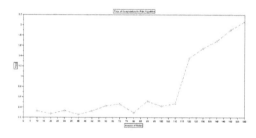

```
Time of Computation for Prim Algorithm

Nodes

   10.
   20.
   30.
   40.
   50.
   60.
   70.
   80.
   90.
  100.
  110.
  120.
  130.
  140.
  150.
  160.


Time for Execution (Respectively)
```

```
0.328125
0.2734375
0.3359375
0.2578125
0.328125
0.4296875
0.4609375
0.296875
0.515625
0.421875
0.46875
1.359375
1.546875
1.6875
1.90625
2.0625
```

2.56   Small Network Routing Performance

```
//Code to compute the CPU time taken by each routing algorithm
   to return the
//Vector of the total distance between each network node and
   the source node and
//Vector composed by the predecessor of each node in order to
   reach the source
//node in respect with the shortest path.
//NOTE: Prim's Algorithm also returns Vector that gathers the
   chronological order
//how network nodes are visited. Refer to documentation for
   details.

//Clear display and environment variables
clc
clear all


disp("For a Small Network Topology with Nodes in the network =
   90 ");
//Creating a random topology which is Small in size
network_size=90;              //network size is 90
net_square_area=1000;             //network square area side is
   1000
locality_radius=100;           //locality radius is 100
[g]=NL_T_LocalityConnex(network_size,net_square_area,
   locality_radius); //generation of a random topology in
   respect with the Locality method.
iteration=NL_F_RandInt1n(length(g.node_x)); //selection of the
   source node
window_index=1;               //window index
g.node_diam(iteration)=40; //node diameter
g.node_border(iteration)=10; //node border
g.node_color(iteration)=5; //node color
[f]=NL_G_ShowGraphN(g,window_index);//graph visualization

//Application of the BFS algorithm
for iteration = 1:10           //Run 10 iterations
   timer();            //Initialize timer
   [dist,pred]=NL_R_BFS(g,iteration); //application of NL_R_BFS
   A(iteration) = timer()     //Store timer value in array
end
average_time=mean(A);           //Calculate average time taken
disp(average_time,"BFS:")       //Display average time

//Application of the Weighted BFS algorithm
```

```
for iteration = 1:10
    timer();
    [dist,pred]=NL_R_BFSWeight(g,iteration);//application of
        NL_R_BFSWeight
    A(iteration) = timer()
end
average_time=mean(A);
disp(average_time, "Weighted BFS:")

//Application of the Bellman-Ford algorithm
for iteration = 1:10
    timer();
    [dist,pred]=NL_R_BellmanFord(g,iteration);//application of
        NL_R_BellmanFord
    A(iteration) = timer()
end
average_time=mean(A);
disp(average_time,"Bellman-Ford:")

//Application of the DFS algorithm
for iteration = 1:10
    timer();
    [dist,pred]=NL_R_DFS(g,iteration);//application of NL_R_DFS
    A(iteration) = timer()
end
average_time=mean(A);
disp(average_time,"DFS:")

//Application of the Weighted DFS algorithm
for iteration = 1:10
    timer();
    [dist,pred]=NL_R_DFSWeight(g,iteration);//application of
        NL_R_DFSWeight
    A(iteration) = timer()
end
average_time=mean(A);
disp(average_time,"Weighted DFS:")

//Application of the Dijkstra algorithm
for iteration = 1:10
    timer();
    [dist,pred]=NL_R_Dijkstra(g,iteration);//application of
        NL_R_Dijkstra
    A(iteration) = timer()
end
average_time=mean(A);
disp(average_time,"Dijkstra:")

//Application of the Floyd-Warshall algorithm
for iteration = 1:10
```

```
   timer();
   [dist,pred]=NL_R_FloydWarshall(g);//application of
       NL_R_FloydWarshall
   A(iteration) = timer()
end
average_time=mean(A);
disp(average_time,"Floyd-Warshall:")

//Application of the Prim's algorithm
for iteration = 1:10
   timer();
   [dist,v,pred]=NL_R_Prim(g,iteration,2,1);//application of
       NL_R_Prim, setting Display Parameter as 2 and window
       index as 1
   A(iteration) = timer()
end
average_time=mean(A);
disp(average_time,"Prim:")
```

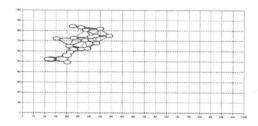

```
For a Small Network Topology with Nodes in the network = 90


 BFS    : 0.0171875
Weighted BFS : 0.01875
Bellman-Ford : 0.015625
DFS    : 0.0109375
Weighted DFS : 0.00625
Dijkstra : 0.0109375
Floyd-Warshall  : 0.0265625
Prim   : 0.671875
```

2.57 Tiny Network Routing Performance

```
//Code to compute the CPU time taken by each routing algorithm
    to return the
//Vector of the total distance between each network node and
    the source node and
//Vector composed by the predecessor of each node in order to
    reach the source
//node in respect with the shortest path.
//NOTE: Prim's Algorithm also returns Vector that gathers the
    chronological order
//how network nodes are visited. Refer to documentation for
    details.

//Clear display and environment variables
clc
clear all


disp("For a Tiny Network Topology with Nodes in the network =
    80 ");
//Creating a random topology which is Tiny in size
network_size=80;                //network size is 80
net_square_area=1000;              //network square area side is
    1000
locality_radius=100;          //locality radius is 100
[g]=NL_T_LocalityConnex(network_size,net_square_area,
    locality_radius); //generation of a random topology in
    respect with the Locality method.
iteration=NL_F_RandInt1n(length(g.node_x)); //selection of the
    source node
window_index=1;                //window index
g.node_diam(iteration)=40; //node diameter
g.node_border(iteration)=10; //node border
g.node_color(iteration)=5; //node color
[f]=NL_G_ShowGraphN(g,window_index);//graph visualization

//Application of the BFS algorithm
for iteration = 1:10           //Run 10 iterations
   timer();             //Initialize timer
   [dist,pred]=NL_R_BFS(g,iteration); //application of NL_R_BFS
   A(iteration) = timer()      //Store timer value in array
end
average_time=mean(A);            //Calculate average time taken
disp(average_time,"BFS:")        //Display average time

//Application of the Weighted BFS algorithm
```

```
for iteration = 1:10
   timer();
   [dist,pred]=NL_R_BFSWeight(g,iteration);//application of
      NL_R_BFSWeight
   A(iteration) = timer()
end
average_time=mean(A);
disp(average_time, "Weighted BFS:")

//Application of the Bellman-Ford algorithm
for iteration = 1:10
   timer();
   [dist,pred]=NL_R_BellmanFord(g,iteration);//application of
      NL_R_BellmanFord
   A(iteration) = timer()
end
average_time=mean(A);
disp(average_time,"Bellman-Ford:")

//Application of the DFS algorithm
for iteration = 1:10
   timer();
   [dist,pred]=NL_R_DFS(g,iteration);//application of NL_R_DFS
   A(iteration) = timer()
end
average_time=mean(A);
disp(average_time,"DFS:")

//Application of the Weighted DFS algorithm
for iteration = 1:10
   timer();
   [dist,pred]=NL_R_DFSWeight(g,iteration);//application of
      NL_R_DFSWeight
   A(iteration) = timer()
end
average_time=mean(A);
disp(average_time,"Weighted DFS:")

//Application of the Dijkstra algorithm
for iteration = 1:10
   timer();
   [dist,pred]=NL_R_Dijkstra(g,iteration);//application of
      NL_R_Dijkstra
   A(iteration) = timer()
end
average_time=mean(A);
disp(average_time,"Dijkstra:")

//Application of the Floyd-Warshall algorithm
for iteration = 1:10
```

```
   timer();
   [dist,pred]=NL_R_FloydWarshall(g);//application of
       NL_R_FloydWarshall
   A(iteration) = timer()
end
average_time=mean(A);
disp(average_time,"Floyd-Warshall:")

//Application of the Prim's algorithm
for iteration = 1:10
   timer();
   [dist,v,pred]=NL_R_Prim(g,iteration,2,1);//application of
       NL_R_Prim, setting Display Parameter as 2 and window
       index as 1
   A(iteration) = timer()
end
average_time=mean(A);
disp(average_time,"Prim:")
```

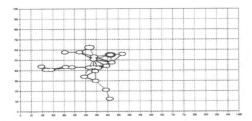

```
For a Tiny Network Topology with Nodes in the network = 80

 BFS   : 0.0203125
Weighted BFS : 0.0078125
Bellman-Ford : 0.0125
DFS    : 0.009375
Weighted DFS : 0.009375
Dijkstra : 0.0078125
Floyd-Warshall  : 0.0296875
Prim   : 0.51875
```

2.58   VeryLarge Network Routing Performance

```
//Code to compute the CPU time taken by each routing algorithm
    to return the
//Vector of the total distance between each network node and
    the source node and
//Vector composed by the predecessor of each node in order to
    reach the source
//node in respect with the shortest path.
//NOTE: Prim's Algorithm also returns Vector that gathers the
    chronological order
//how network nodes are visited. Refer to documentation for
    details.

//Clear display and environment variables
clc
clear all


disp("For a Very Large Network Topology with Nodes in the
    network = 180 ");
//Creating a random topology which is Very Large in size
network_size=180;              //network size is 180
net_square_area=1000;              //network square area side is
    1000
locality_radius=100;            //locality radius is 100
[g]=NL_T_LocalityConnex(network_size,net_square_area,
    locality_radius); //generation of a random topology in
    respect with the Locality method.
iteration=NL_F_RandInt1n(length(g.node_x)); //selection of the
    source node
window_index=1;                //window index
g.node_diam(iteration)=40; //node diameter
g.node_border(iteration)=10; //node border
g.node_color(iteration)=5; //node color
[f]=NL_G_ShowGraphN(g,window_index);//graph visualization

//Application of the BFS algorithm
for iteration = 1:10              //Run 10 iterations
   timer();            //Initialize timer
   [dist,pred]=NL_R_BFS(g,iteration); //application of NL_R_BFS
   A(iteration) = timer()      //Store timer value in array
end
average_time=mean(A);              //Calculate average time taken
disp(average_time,"BFS:")        //Display average time

//Application of the Weighted BFS algorithm
```

```
for iteration = 1:10
   timer();
   [dist,pred]=NL_R_BFSWeight(g,iteration);//application of
        NL_R_BFSWeight
   A(iteration) = timer()
end
average_time=mean(A);
disp(average_time, "Weighted BFS:")

//Application of the Bellman-Ford algorithm
for iteration = 1:10
   timer();
   [dist,pred]=NL_R_BellmanFord(g,iteration);//application of
        NL_R_BellmanFord
   A(iteration) = timer()
end
average_time=mean(A);
disp(average_time,"Bellman-Ford:")

//Application of the DFS algorithm
for iteration = 1:10
   timer();
   [dist,pred]=NL_R_DFS(g,iteration);//application of NL_R_DFS
   A(iteration) = timer()
end
average_time=mean(A);
disp(average_time,"DFS:")

//Application of the Weighted DFS algorithm
for iteration = 1:10
   timer();
   [dist,pred]=NL_R_DFSWeight(g,iteration);//application of
        NL_R_DFSWeight
   A(iteration) = timer()
end
average_time=mean(A);
disp(average_time,"Weighted DFS:")

//Application of the Dijkstra algorithm
for iteration = 1:10
   timer();
   [dist,pred]=NL_R_Dijkstra(g,iteration);//application of
        NL_R_Dijkstra
   A(iteration) = timer()
end
average_time=mean(A);
disp(average_time,"Dijkstra:")

//Application of the Floyd-Warshall algorithm
for iteration = 1:10
```

```
   timer();
   [dist,pred]=NL_R_FloydWarshall(g);//application of
       NL_R_FloydWarshall
   A(iteration) = timer()
end
average_time=mean(A);
disp(average_time,"Floyd-Warshall:")

//Application of the Prim's algorithm
for iteration = 1:10
   timer();
   [dist,v,pred]=NL_R_Prim(g,iteration,2,1);//application of
       NL_R_Prim, setting Display Parameter as 2 and window
       index as 1
   A(iteration) = timer()
end
average_time=mean(A);
disp(average_time,"Prim:")
```

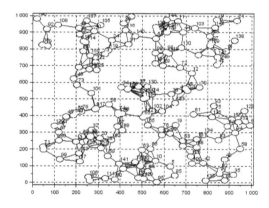

```
For a Very Large Network Topology with Nodes in the network =
    180

BFS    : 0.140625
Weighted BFS : 0.065625
Bellman-Ford : 0.9640625
DFS    : 0.0734375
Weighted DFS : 0.06875
Dijkstra : 0.084375
Floyd-Warshall  : 10.210938
Prim   : 3.56875
```

2.59 Shortest Path Using Dijikitras

```
a=[0.3 0.3 0.3 0.3];//first parameter of the Waxman model for
    each network layer
b=[0.9 0.7 0.5 0.3];//second parameter of the Waxman model for
    each network layer
nl=[30 50 50 100];//quantity of nodes per network layer
l=[1000 150 100 40];//squared area side per network layer
n=[3 5 3 3];//maximal quantity of nodes per subnetwork for each
    layer
s=4;//quantity of network layers
db=20;//original diameter of nodes
dd=15;//diameter difference between successive network layers
cv=[2 5 6 1];//color of each network layer
[g,d,nl]=NL_T_MultiLevel(a,b,nl,l,n,s,db,dd,cv);//application
    of NL_T_MultiLevel
ind=1;//window index
f=NL_G_ShowGraph(g,ind);//graph visualization
[f]=NL_G_ShowGraphN(g,ind);//graph visualization
[dist,pred]=NL_R_Dijkstra(g,1);//application of NL_R_Dijkstra
dist(1:10)//first ten values
pred(1:10)//first ten values
```

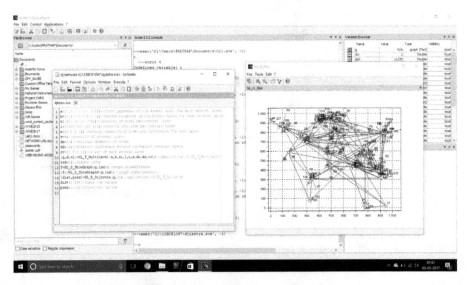

Figure 2.24: Shortest path using Dijikitras

2.60   Shortest Path Using Prims

```
a=[0.3 0.3 0.3 0.3];//first parameter of the Waxman model for
    each network layer
b=[0.9 0.7 0.5 0.3];//second parameter of the Waxman model for
    each network layer
nl=[30 50 50 100];//quantity of nodes per network layer
l=[1000 150 100 40];//squared area side per network layer
n=[3 5 3 3];//maximal quantity of nodes per subnetwork for each
    layer
s=4;//quantity of network layers
db=20;//original diameter of nodes
dd=15;//diameter difference between successive network layers
cv=[2 5 6 1];//color of each network layer
[g,d,nl]=NL_T_MultiLevel(a,b,nl,l,n,s,db,dd,cv);//application
    of NL_T_MultiLevel
ind=1;//window index
f=NL_G_ShowGraph(g,ind);//graph visualization
[f]=NL_G_ShowGraphN(g,ind);//graph visualization
dw=2;//display parameter
ind=1;//window index
[go,v,pred]=NL_R_Prim(g,i,dw,ind)//application of NL_R_Prim
```

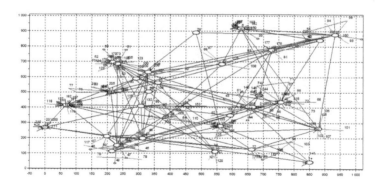

Figure 2.25: Finding path using Prims

2.61   Circle Place Comparison

```
clc;
n=150;//original network size
L=1000;//network square area side
dmax=100;//Locality radius
[g]=NtgLocalityConnex(n,L,dmax);//generation of a topology in
    respect with the Locality method
gn=length(g.node_x);//real network size
i=Random(gn);//selection of the central node
N=10;//quantity of new nodes
d=50;//disc radius
[ge]=CirclePlace(N,d,g,i);//application of CirclePlace
ge.edge_color=[ones(1,length(g.head)) 5*ones(1,N)];//display
    the union graph
ge.edge_width=[ones(1,length(g.head)) 1.5*ones(1,N)];
ge.node_color=[ones(1,length(g.node_x)) 5*ones(1,N)];
//ge.node_color(i)=2;
//ge.node_border=[ones(1,length(g.node_x)) 1.5*ones(1,N)];
//ge.node_border(i)=2;
show_graph(ge);
```

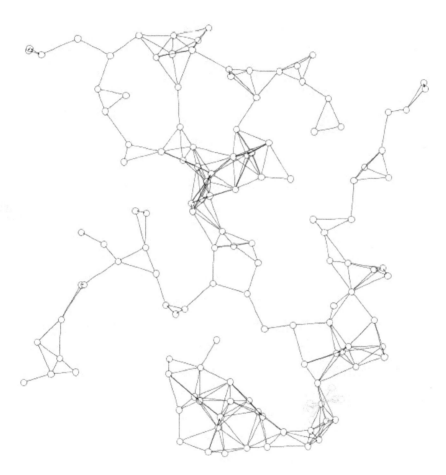

Figure 2.26: Circle Place Comparison

2.62   Comparison of Dijikstra and Prims

```
n=150;//network size
L=1000;//network square area side
dmax=100;//Locality radius
//generation of a topology in respect with the Locality method
[g]=NtgLocalityConnex(n,L,dmax);

/////Djkstrs Routing Algorithm
nf=length(g.node_x);//real network size
nl=length(g.head);//quantity of network links
[i,j]=Random_i_j(nf);//selection of the extremal nodes
[path]=RoutingDijkstra(g,'arc',i,j);//application of
    RoutingDijkstra
p=nodes_2_path(path,g);
EC=ones(1,nl);//display the path between i and j
EB=ones(1,nl);
EC(p)=5;
EB(p)=2;
D=ones(1,nf);
D(path)=3;
g.node_border=D;
g.edge_color=EC;
g.edge_width=EB;
show_graph(g);
path


//////////Prims Algorithm Performed in the Same Graph
    ////////////////
dmax=100;//Locality radius
i=Random(length(g.node_x));//selection of the source node
dw=2;//display parameter
[v,pred]=RoutingPrim(g,i,dw);//application of RoutingPrim
v
pred
```

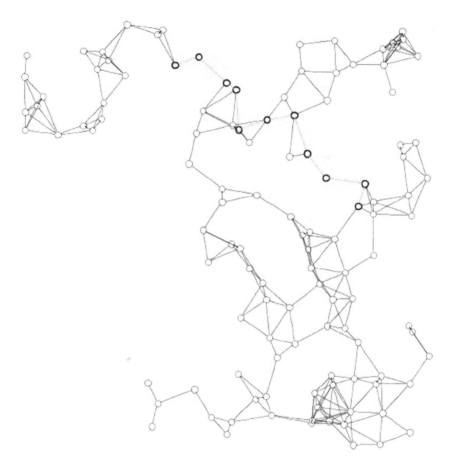

Figure 2.27: Comparison of Dijikstra and Prims

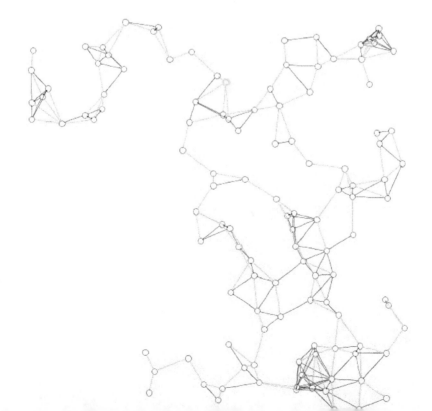

2.63   Analysis of Dijikstra

```
a=0.1;//first parameter of the Waxman model
b=0.8;//second parameter of the Waxman model
n=1000;//network size
l=10000000;//network squared area side
[g,d]=NL_T_Waxman(a,b,n,l);//application of NL_T_Waxman
ind=1;//window index
i=NL_F_RandInt1n(length(g.node_x));//selection of the source
    node
ind=1;//window index
g.node_diam(i)=40;//node diameter
g.node_border(i)=10;//node border
g.node_color(i)=5;//node color
[f]=NL_G_ShowGraphN(g,ind);//graph visualization
[dist,pred]=NL_R_Dijkstra(g,i);//application of NL_R_Dijkstra
dist(1:10)//first ten values
pred(1:10)//first ten values
```

2.64   Edgelength

```
n=50;//network size
L=1000;//network square area side
dmax=100;//locality radius
[g]=NtgLocalityConnex(n,L,dmax);//generation of a random
    topology in respect with the Locality method.
show_graph(g);
g.edges.data.length=[]
[g]=EdgeLength(g);//application of EdgeLength
g.edges.data.length
```

2.65   Enhanced Routing Table Vs Shortest Routing Table

```
//Enhanced Routing Table
load('./demos/RoutingTables_topo_100_1.dat');//loading of the
    network routing tables
[g]=load_graph('./demos/topo_100_1.graph')
rt1=[rt1(:,1) rt1(:,3:$)];//shape of the normal routing table
[ert]=EnhancedRoutingTable(rt1,g);//application of
    EnhancedRoutingTable
```

```
rt1(1:10,:)
ert(1:10,:)

//Shortest Routing Table
[l c]=size(rt1);//size of the routing table rt1
rt=[rt1 zeros(l,2)];//addition of two empty columns
rt(1:10,:)//initial state
[rt]=RoutingShortestRT(rt);//application of RoutingShortestRT
rt(1:10,:)//final state
```

2.66   Euclidean Distance

```
n=80;//network size
L=1000;//network square area side
dmax=100;//locality radius
[g]=NtgLocalityConnex(n,L,dmax);//generation of a random
    topology in respect with the Locality method.
N=length(g.node_x);//real network size
[n1,n2]=Random_i_j(N);//selection of two distinct nodes
nd=ones(1,n);//display the graph
nc=ones(1,n);
nd([n1 n2])=3;
nc([n1 n2])=5;
g.node_border=nd;
g.node_color=nc;
show_graph(g);
[d]=Distance(n1,n2,g.node_x,g.node_y);//application of Distance
n1
n2
d
```

2.67   NTG Locality Connex

```
n=100;//network size
l=1000;//network squared area side
d=100;//Locality radius

[g]=NtgLocalityConnex(n,l,d);//application of NtgLocalityConnex
[g1]=NtgLocality(n,l,d);//application of NtgLocality

show_graph(g1);
show_graph(g);
```

2.68 NTG Waxmann Comparison

```
a=0.1;//first parameter of the Waxman model
b=0.8;//second parameter of the Waxman model
n=100;//network size
l=1000;//network squared area side

//application of NtgWaxmanConnex
[g]=NtgWaxmanConnex(a,b,n,l);
show_graph(g);

//NTGWaxMan
[g1,d]=NtgWaxman(a,b,n,l);//application of NtgWaxman
show_graph(g1);
scf(1);clf(1);
plot(d);
plot2d3(d);
xtitle('','node index','degree');
```

2.69 Rounting Table Optimisation of Djkstrs

```
n=80;//network size
l=1000;//network squared area side
d=100;//Locality radius
[g]=NtgLocalityConnex(n,l,d);//generation of a topology
show_graph(g);
[rt2]=RoutingTableDijkstra(g);//application of
    RoutingTableDijkstra

///using shortest rounting table (Routing Shortest Rt)

rt=[rt2 zeros(l,2)];//addition of two empty columns
rt(1:10,:)//initial state
[rt]=RoutingShortestRT(rt);//application of RoutingShortestRT
rt(1:10,:)//final state
rt
```

2.70 Rounting Table BellmanFord

```
n=80;//network size
l=1000;//network squared area side
d=100;//Locality radius
[g]=NtgLocalityConnex(n,l,d);//generation of a topology
```

```
show_graph(g);
TTL=10;//Flood Time-To-Live
[rt]=RoutingTableFlood(g,TTL);//application of
    RoutingTableFlood
rt
i=Random(length(g.node_x));//selection of the source node
EB=ones(1,length(g.node_x));//display the source node
EC=ones(1,length(g.node_x));
EB(i)=3;
EC(i)=5;
g.node_border=EB;
g.node_color=EC;
show_graph(g);
[dist,pred]=RoutingBellmanFord(g,i);//Application of
    RoutingBellmanFord
i
dist
pred
```

2.71   Rounting BFS and DFS

```
n=150;//network size
L=1000;//network square area side
dmax=100;//Locality radius
[g]=NtgLocalityConnex(n,L,dmax);//generation of a topology in
    respect with the Locality method
i=Random(length(g.node_x));//selection of the source node
dw=6;//display parameter
[v,pred]=RoutingBFSWeight(g,i,dw);//application of
    RoutingBFSWeight
v
pred
```

```
//DEPTH FIRST SEARCH
i=Random(length(g.node_x));//selection of the source node
dw=2;//display parameter
[v,pred]=RoutingDFS(g,i,dw);//application of RoutingDFS
v
pred
```

2.72   Vector Operation

```
v=[1 2 3 4 2 4 4 5];//original vector
```

```
//Difference Between Vectors
disp('Given Vector');
v


disp('Reversing Vector');
//Reversing Vector
[vi]=RVector(v);//application of RVector
v
vi

disp('Removing 3 from Vector');
//Removing Value From Vector

vl=3;//value
[v]=Remov(v,vl);//application of Remov
vl
v


//unity in Vector

disp('Unity Application');

[nv]=Unity(v);//application of Unity
v
nv
```

2.73   Weight Graph

```
n=90;     //network size
L=500;      //network square area side
dmax=100;     //locality radius
[g]=NtgLocalityConnex(n,L,dmax);   //generation of a random
    topology in respect with the Locality method.
show_graph(g);
g.edges.data.length=[]
[g]=EdgeLength(g);        //application of EdgeLength
g.edges.data.length
```

Chapter 3

VISUALIZATION THROUGH NARVAL

3.1 Visualization

```
clc;
gdate=getdate();
seed=gdate(10);
rand('seed',seed);//initialization of the random values
    generator
number_of_obstacle=5;//quantity of obstacles (rectangle)
squared_area=1000;//squared area side
min_height=150;//minimal height
max_height=150;//maximal height
min_width=100;//minimal width
max_width=100;//maximal width
avail_angles=[0 %pi/2 %pi -%pi/2];//available angles for
    obstacles
[X_cooridate_of_corners,Y_cooridate_of_corners,
    X_cooridates_of_corners,Y_cooridates_of_corners,H,W,A]=
    NL_V_RectanglesCorners(number_of_obstacle,squared_area,
    min_height,max_height,min_width,max_width);//generation of
    obstacles
Potential_rectangles=NL_V_PotentialRectangles(
    X_cooridates_of_corners,Y_cooridates_of_corners,H,W,A,
    squared_area);//generation of obstacle matrix
zoom_factor=10;//zoom factor
obstacle_matrix=2;// 1=mean, 2=max, 3=min, 4=median
Potential_scale_modifier=NL_V_MRA(Potential_rectangles,
    zoom_factor,obstacle_matrix);//scale modification
[Potential_scale_modifier_x,Potential_scale_modifier_y]=size(
    Potential_scale_modifier);//image size
```

```
window_index1=1;//window index
window_index2=2;//window index
scf(window_index1);
clf(window_index1);
grayplot(1:Potential_scale_modifier_x,1:
    Potential_scale_modifier_y,Potential_scale_modifier);//graph
    visualization
xset("colormap",graycolormap(128));
scf(window_index2);
clf(window_index2);
[PEz]=NL_V_Erosion(Potential_scale_modifier);//contour
    performance
Contour=Potential_scale_modifier-PEz;//contour 1
[Countourx,Countoury]=size(Contour);//image size
grayplot(1:Countourx,1:Countoury,Contour);//graph visualization
xset("colormap",graycolormap(128));
window_index3=3;//window index
scf(window_index3);
clf(window_index3);
[Dimension]=NL_V_DistanceMapObject(Potential_scale_modifier,
    Contour);//creation of the distance map
[Dimensionx,Dimensiony]=size(Dimension);//image size
grayplot(1:Dimensionx,1:Dimensiony,Dimension);//graph
    visualization
xset("colormap",graycolormap(128));
Kernel1=[0 -1 0;-1 4 -1;0 -1 0];//kernel 1
Kernel2=[-1 -1 -1;-1 8 -1;-1 -1 -1];//kernel 2
[Dimension1]=NL_V_Convolution2D(Dimension,Kernel2);
[Dimension1x,Dimension1y]=size(Dimension1);//image size
window_index4=4;
scf(window_index4);
clf(window_index4);
grayplot(1:Dimension1x,1:Dimension1y,Dimension1);//graph
    visualization
xset("colormap",graycolormap(128));
min_width=3;//kernel size
[cornerz]=NL_V_Moravec(Potential_scale_modifier,min_width);//
    corner detection
Threshold=(max(cornerz)+min(cornerz))/2;//threshold
[cornerT]=NL_V_MoravecFilter(cornerz,Threshold);//remove false
    detection
[cornerTx,cornerTy]=size(cornerT);//image size
window_index5=5;//window index
scf(window_index5);
clf(window_index5);
grayplot(1:squared_area/zoom_factor,1:squared_area/zoom_factor,
    cornerT);//graph visualization
xset("colormap",graycolormap(128));
[x_axis,y_axis,direction,length_vector]=NL_V_ContourCorners(
    Contour);//Corners detection
```

```
Correlation_mode=2;//parameters
Min_dist_bw_corners=3;
Threshold_corel=1;
Threshold_gradient=1;
[Updated_x-coordinate_of_corners,Updated_y-
    coordinate_of_corners,ns]=NL_V_ContourCornersFilt(x_axis,
    y_axis,direction,length_vector,Correlation_mode,
    Threshold_corel,Threshold_gradient,Min_dist_bw_corners);//
    remove false detections
Infinite_potential_value=100000;
[potential_matrix]=NL_V_PotentialField(Potential_scale_modifier
    ,Infinite_potential_value);//performance of the potential
    field
[lPotential_scale_modifier,cPotential_scale_modifier]=size(
    Potential_scale_modifier)
x_axis=2;//origine
y_axis=2;
xg=lPotential_scale_modifier-1;//destination: first diagonal
yg=cPotential_scale_modifier-1;
[X_coordinates_of_all_pixels_in_path,
    y_coordinates_of_all_pixels_in_path]=NL_V_PotentialFieldPath
    (x_axis,y_axis,xg,yg,potential_matrix); //application of
    NL_V_PotentialFieldPath
Potetial_field_pathl=Potential_scale_modifier;
for first_k_value=1:length(X_coordinates_of_all_pixels_in_path)
Potetial_field_pathl(X_coordinates_of_all_pixels_in_path(
    first_k_value),y_coordinates_of_all_pixels_in_path(
    first_k_value))=2;
end
window_index6=6;//window index
scf(window_index6);
clf(window_index6);
grayplot(1:lPotential_scale_modifier,1:lPotential_scale_odifier
    ,Potetial_field_pathl);//graph visualization
xset("colormap",graycolormap(128));
window_index7=7;//window index
scf(window_index7);
clf(window_index7);
[lCountour_matrix,cCountour_matrix]=size(Contour);//image size
Image_contour=zeros(lCountour_matrix,cCountour_matrix);
for k_value_update=1:length(Updated_x-coordinate_of_corners)
Image_contour(Updated_x-coordinate_of_corners(k_value_update),
    Updated_y-coordinate_of_corners(k_value_update))=1;
end
grayplot(1:squared_area/zoom_factor,1:squared_area/zoom_factor,
    Image_contour);//graph visualization
xset("colormap",graycolormap(128));
[Graph]=NL_V_VisibilityGraph(Updated_x-coordinate_of_corners,
    Updated_y-coordinate_of_corners,ns,Potential_scale_modifier)
    ;//application of NL_V_VisibilityGraph
```

```
window_index8=8;//window index
Graph.node_x=Graph.node_x*zoom_factor;
Graph.node_y=Graph.node_y*zoom_factor;
NL_G_ShowGraph(Graph,window_index8);//graph visualization
```

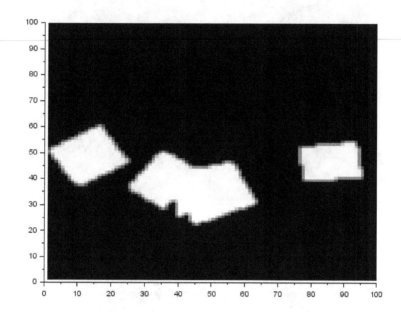

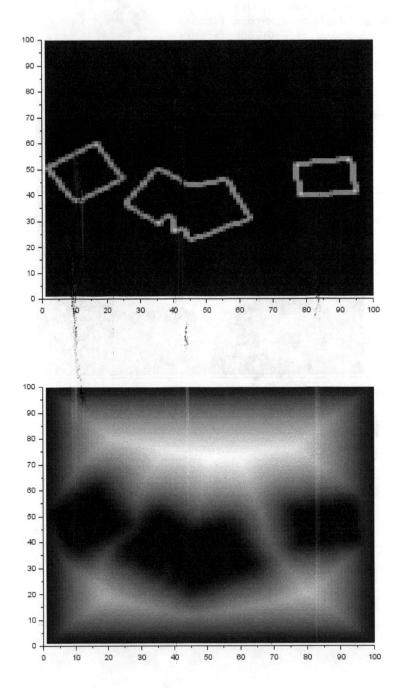

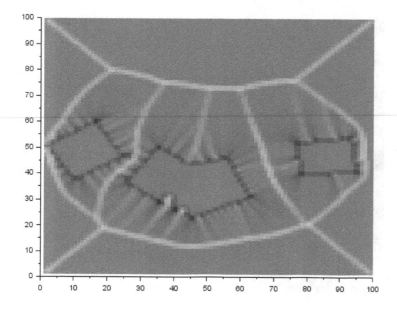

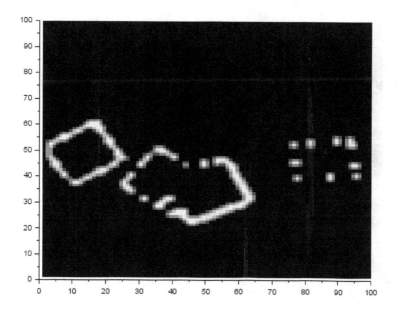

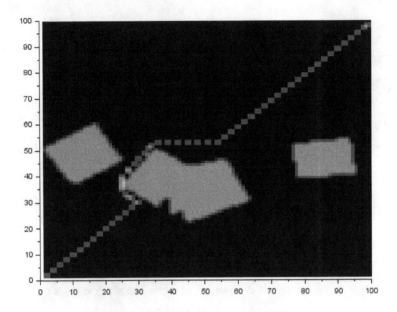

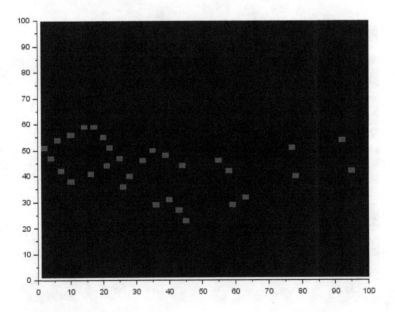

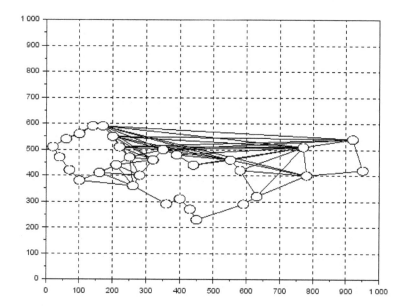